School Subject-Integrated Reading Series

# Reading for Subject

**SECOND EDITION**

**3**

SECOND EDITION

# Reading for Subject 3

**Publisher** Chung Kyudo
**Authors** Ko Miseon, Kim Seungmi, Kim Haeja, Yu Sunyeh,
          Han Jiyoung, Rachel Somer
**Editors** Jeong Yeonsoon, Seo Jeong-ah
**Designer** Koo Soojung

First published in December 2021
By Darakwon, Inc.
Darakwon Bldg., 211, Munbal-ro, Paju-si, Gyeonggi-do 10881
Republic of Korea
Tel: 82-2-736-2031 (Ext. 250)
Fax: 82-2-732-2037

**ISBN** 978-89-277-0898-8 54740
       978-89-277-0895-7 54740 (set)

**www.darakwon.co.kr**

**Photo Credits**
Matyas Rehak (p.11), travelview (p.18), Pablo Rogat (p.19),
Robcartorres (p.22), christianthiel.net (p.23), asobov (p.34), Claude
Huot (p.42), neftali (p.43), IngeBlessas (p.50), JackKPhoto (p.54),
dmitro2009 (p.63), Anton_Ivanov (p.66), Giuliano Del Moretto
(p.78), Igor Bulgarin (p.79), 360b (p.91), thipjang (p.103), Pavel
Kirichenko (p.106) / www.shutterstock.com
NASA_Dragonfly_mission_to_Titan.jpg (p.31) / https://
ko.m.wikipedia.org/wiki/
*AC85.Aℓ194L.1869 pt.2aa, Houghton Library, Harvard University
(p.71) / https://commons.wikimedia.org/wiki/

**Components** Main Book / Workbook
9 8 7 6 5 4 3       23 24 25 26 27

School Subject-Integrated Reading Series

# Reading for Subject

SECOND EDITION

**3**

# How to Use This Book

This book has 5 chapters, and each consists of 4 units. At the end of a chapter, there is a writing activity with a topic related to the last unit.

## Student Book

QR code for listening to the reading passage

Finding the topic of each paragraph

Two warm-up questions to encourage students to think about the topic of the unit

### BEFORE YOU READ

Students can learn the meaning of key vocabulary words by matching the words with their definitions.

Background knowledge about the topic is provided to help students better understand the main reading passage.

### MAIN READING PASSAGE

Interesting, informative nonfiction reading passages covering various school subjects are provided.

### CHECK YOUR COMPREHENSION

This section asks students to identify the main ideas and details and to make accurate inferences from the passage through 4 multiple-choice and 2 short-answer questions.

### SHOW YOUR COMPREHENSION

Students can remember what they have read and organize the key information in the passage in a visual manner.

### SUMMARIZE YOUR READING

Students can review and practice summarizing the key information in the passage.

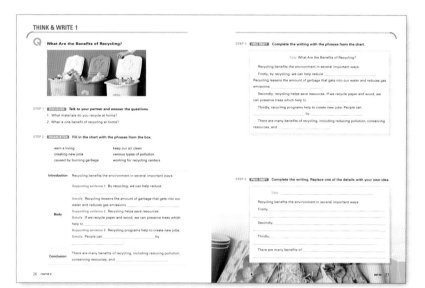

## THINK & WRITE

Students can strengthen their writing skills by connecting ideas from the passage to their own lives. This also helps students prepare themselves for English performance assessments in school.

## Workbook

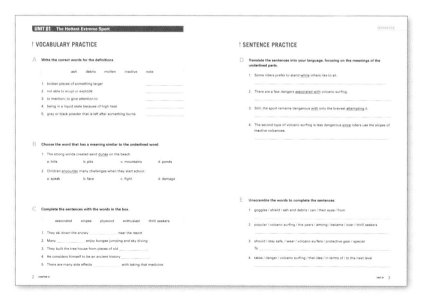

Students can review the vocabulary they learn in each unit. They can also review key structures in the passages by translating sentences and by putting words in the correct order.

# Table of Contents

# CHAPTER
# 01

# UNIT 01

**Subject** Social Studies
**Topic** Volcano Surfing

# The Hottest Extreme Sport

**WARM UP**

1. Do you prefer team sports or extreme sports? Why?
2. What extreme sports would you like to try?

## BEFORE YOU READ

**A** **Match the words with the definitions below.**

1. _____ inspire
2. _____ active
3. _____ lava
4. _____ hike
5. _____ gear
6. _____ shield

a. likely to erupt or explode
b. hot liquid rock from a volcano
c. to block; to protect something
d. clothing or items used to do an activity
e. to take a long walk, usually through nature
f. to cause or lead to the creation of something else

**B** **Background Knowledge**

A volcano is an opening in the Earth's crust. Volcanoes can be either active or inactive. In an active state, lava, volcanic ash, and gases may escape. Some volcanoes have frequent small eruptions. Others have less frequent, large explosions that can endanger the surrounding towns and wildlife.

Volcano surfing is an extreme sport that was **inspired** by sandboarding. In sandboarding, an athlete rides a board down a sand dune. Volcano surfing takes that idea to the next level in terms of danger. Instead of sand dunes, riders board down the slopes of a
5  volcano through volcanic ash.

Zoltan Istvan, an American journalist and extreme sports enthusiast, claims he invented volcano surfing. He did so while visiting Mount Yasur in *Vanuatu in 2002. He notes that there are two types of volcano surfing. The first is when a rider boards down
10  the slope of an **active** volcano. In this case, riders may encounter several dangers, including molten **lava** and volcanic gases. The second type of volcano surfing is less dangerous since riders use the slopes of inactive volcanoes.

Volcano surfing became popular among thrill seekers over
15  the years. Most volcano surfing takes place on Cerro Negro in *Nicaragua. The sport also remains popular on Mount Yasur. Like Cerro Negro, Mount Yasur is an active volcano. Volcano surfers must first **hike** up the slopes. Then they slide down on a thin piece of plywood or metal. Some riders prefer to stand while others like
20  to sit.

There are a few dangers associated with volcano surfing. These include breathing in volcanic gases, being hit by flying lava, and getting injured by sharp rocks. To stay safe, volcano surfers should wear special protective **gear**. Goggles can **shield** their eyes from
25  ash and debris. In addition, jumpsuits can help protect their skin from cuts and burns. Still, the sport remains dangerous with only the bravest attempting it.   Words 265

***Vanuatu**  a country in the South Pacific Ocean that is made up of around 80 islands

***Nicaragua**  a country in Central America located between the Pacific Ocean and the Caribbean Sea

**Q**
**What is the paragraph mainly about?**

P1 What _____ is

P2 The two (features / types) of volcano surfing

P3 Where and (how / when) volcano surfing takes place

P4 The _____ of volcano surfing

# CHECK YOUR COMPREHENSION

**Choose the best answers.**

Main idea

**1** **What is the main idea of the passage?**

    a. Zoltan Istvan created volcano surfing in 2002.

    b. Volcano surfing is a dangerous extreme sport.

    c. The most common type of surfing happens on volcanoes.

    d. Some countries have the best mountains for volcano surfing.

Details

**2** **The type of volcano surfing is determined by whether the volcano is** _____.

    a. active

    b. old

    c. high

    d. common

**3** **According to the passage, which is NOT true about volcano surfing?**

    a. Volcano surfers have to hike up the slopes.

    b. Riders have to sit when they board down the slopes.

    c. Riders can board down the slopes of active volcanoes.

    d. Riders can encounter dangerous gases on active volcanoes.

**4** **What can be inferred from the passage?**

    a. Some riders get burned while volcano surfing.

    b. Zoltan Istvan no longer attempts to volcano surf.

    c. Sandboarding is just as dangerous as volcano surfing.

    d. Riders prefer Cerro Negro to Mount Yasur because it is active.

**Write the answers in complete sentences.**

**5** **How do riders get down the slopes of a volcano?**

_____

**6** **Why do some riders wear goggles?**

_____

# SHOW YOUR COMPREHENSION

**Fill in the chart with the phrases from the box.**

| Volcano Surfing | |
|---|---|
| **How to Do It** | • ❶_____ of a volcano<br>• board down the slopes ❷_____ on plywood or metal |
| **Where to Do It** | • takes place on Cerro Negro and Mount Yasur<br>• riders board down the slopes of ❸_____ or use inactive volcanoes |
| **Dangers** | • breathing in gases, ❹_____, getting injured by sharp rocks<br>• protective gear: goggles shield eyes and ❺_____ |

hike up the slopes    jumpsuits protect skin
being hit by lava    through volcanic ash    an active volcano

# SUMMARIZE YOUR READING

**Complete the summary with the words from the box.**

invented    boards down    metal    sharp rocks
thrill seekers    extreme sport    protective gear    dangerous

Volcano surfing is a(n) ❶_____. American journalist Zoltan Istvan claims he ❷_____ the sport in 2002. There are two types of volcano surfing. The first occurs when a rider ❸_____ an active volcano. The other happens on the slopes of inactive volcanoes, which are less ❹_____. ❺_____ enjoy volcano surfing on Cerro Negro and Mount Yasur. First, they hike up the slopes of the volcano. Then they board down on a piece of plywood or ❻_____. They wear special ❼_____, such as goggles and jumpsuits. These protect them from dangerous gases, flying lava, and ❽_____.

# Plants Have Skills

WARM UP

1. What plants have a bad smell?
2. Why do you think these plants smell bad?

Passion flower ▶

## BEFORE YOU READ

**A   Match the words with the definitions below.**

1. _____ adjust
2. _____ repel
3. _____ trait
4. _____ predator
5. _____ pollination
6. _____ odor

a. to keep someone or something away

b. a smell, especially an unpleasant one

c. to become used to a new situation

d. an animal that eats other living things

e. a particular quality that someone or something has

f. the process of giving pollen to plants to make seeds

**B   Background Knowledge**

Most plants with flowers produce pollen. Pollen is transferred from one plant to another. This allows the plants to produce seeds. These seeds will later become new plants. Insects such as bees, flies, and beetles help with pollination. They carry pollen from flower to flower.

Plants have special ways of surviving. They have great adaptation skills. They respond to changes in their environments and **adjust** to these new conditions. Additionally, plants have developed various systems to increase their chances of survival.
5 These systems help plants attract or **repel** insects. They also help them protect themselves.

Mimicry is one of these systems. Plants use mimicry to copy the **traits** of things around them. They take on the forms, colors and scents of other things to avoid **predators** or to attract insects
10 to make seeds. Some plants imitate other organisms. For instance, flowers that do not have nectar use mimicry for **pollination**. Mimicry helps them resemble nearby flowers that have nectar. Insects are attracted to the flowers and then pollinate them. Some kinds of orchids are examples of this.

15 Other plants survive by imitating their surroundings. They use mimicry to look just like the environment around them. In this manner, they can hide from attackers. For instance, lithops are found among stones. They hide themselves in their environment by resembling the stones around them. This keeps them safe from
20 predators.

Scents made by plants can also be used to defend against or to attract insects. One type of passion flower gives off a unique smell. It makes butterflies believe the plant is rotten or in bad condition. Through this, the plant prevents butterflies from laying eggs on its
25 leaves. On the other hand, some plants make an **odor** that helps them get pollinated. The western skunk cabbage has an odor like that of a skunk. This odor attracts pollinators like flies and beetles.

Words 266

Q
**What is the paragraph mainly about?**
P1 Ways plants (adapt / consume) to survive

P2 How _____ works in plants

P3 How plants (imitate / change) their surroundings

P4 How _____ help plants survive

Lithops ▶

# CHECK YOUR COMPREHENSION

Choose the best answers.

<u>Main idea</u>  **1**  **What is the passage mainly about?**

    a. Special skills used by plants to survive

    b. How plants adjust to their environments

    c. The environments plants can survive in

    d. The importance of plant adaptation skills

<u>Details</u>  **2**  **Which is NOT mentioned as a method plants use to survive?**

    a. Imitating other plants

    b. Looking like their surroundings

    c. Having sharp thorns or leaves

    d. Producing unpleasant smells

**3**  **Why does the author mention orchids?**

    a. To describe how the plants look

    b. To explain how insects help plants pollinate

    c. To emphasize how important mimicry is to plants

    d. To give an example of some plants that imitate other plants

**4**  **Lithops use mimicry** _____.

    a. to repel insects

    b. to trap prey

    c. to avoid predators

    d. to attract pollinators

Write the answers in complete sentences.

**5**  **How does the smell of passion flowers affect butterflies?**

_____

**6**  **Why does the western skunk cabbage give off an odor?**

_____

# SHOW YOUR COMPREHENSION

**Fill in the chart with the phrases from the box.**

| Mimicry in Plants | |
|---|---|
| **Plants Imitating Other Organisms** | • Orchids: look like flowers that have nectar<br>  – attract insects that ❶_____ |
| **Plants Resembling ❷_____** | • Lithops: resemble ❸_____ to hide from attackers |
| **Plants Using Scents** | • Passion flowers: ❹_____ to keep butterflies away<br>• Western skunk cabbages: have an odor to<br>  ❺_____ |

the stones around them     pollinate the flowers

their surroundings     attract pollinators     give off a unique smell

# SUMMARIZE YOUR READING

**Complete the summary with the words from the box.**

imitate     mimicry     attract insects     gives off

certain smells     pollination     adaptation     adjust to

Plants are able to survive by using ❶_____ skills. They respond to environmental changes and ❷_____ these new conditions. They also ❸_____ the forms, colors, and scents of nearby things. This special skill is called ❹_____. Some types of orchids use mimicry. Although they do not have nectar, they resemble plants that ❺_____. These insects then help with ❻_____. Similarly, lithops can hide from attackers by resembling their surroundings. Other plants, like some passion flowers, make ❼_____ that keep butterflies from laying eggs on their leaves. In addition, the western skunk cabbage ❽_____ an odor to attract pollinators.

# Born with a Destiny

1. What are social classes?
2. Do you think people are treated equally in your country?

## BEFORE YOU READ

**A   Match the words with the definitions below.**

1. _____ status          a. a job or profession

2. _____ rural           b. someone who buys and sells goods

3. _____ occupation      c. one's social or professional position

4. _____ interact        d. far away from large towns or cities

5. _____ merchant        e. someone who is not accepted by a group or society

6. _____ outcast         f. to communicate with others or to spend time together

**B   Background Knowledge**

India's social system is called a caste system. It is one of the oldest in the world, dating back to 1200 BCE. Although it still deeply affects the lives of modern-day Indians, there are now laws to prevent discrimination against those of lower castes. Despite these laws, some Indians still experience discrimination.

A caste system is a social structure that divides people into groups. Each group has a different social **status** and role in society. Many times, the way people are viewed and treated by others depends on their castes. Different forms of the caste system have been found in various cultures. A caste system even continues to exist in India today.

The caste system in modern India is more prominent in **rural** areas than in urban ones. The term caste describes two Indian social concepts, *jati* and *varna*. Indian society is divided into numerous communities called *jatis*. Each *jati* belongs to a different status group called a *varna*. In India, the people in each *varna* have certain roles or **occupations** in society. In addition, they only **interact** with and marry others from the same caste. People do not choose what caste they belong to but are born into one.

Originally, there were four main *varnas* in India. The Brahmins, the highest rank, were the teachers and priests. The Kshatriyas were the soldiers, rulers, and landlords. The Vaishyas were the **merchants** and farmers who owned their own farms. The Sudras were the servants and workers. Later, the fifth group, the Untouchables, was added.

The Untouchables were the lowest rank. They were not part of the original four *varnas*. Instead, they were considered **outcasts** from society. Most of them lived in poverty and were treated badly by others. People even avoided physical contact with them because they were considered to be polluted. In modern India, there are laws to protect the Untouchables, but many are still discriminated against. **Words 265**

Q
**What is the paragraph mainly about?**

P1 What a _____ is

P2 How India's caste system (started / works)

P3 How Indian society was divided into _____

P4 How the Untouchables were (educated / treated)

# CHECK YOUR COMPREHENSION

Choose the best answers.

Main idea  1  **What is the passage mainly about?**

    a. The caste system in India

    b. Different forms of the caste system

    c. How the Untouchables are treated in India

    d. The effects of the caste system on modern India

Details  2  **According to the passage, which is NOT true about India's caste system?**

    a. A person's caste is decided by birth.

    b. Rural people are less strict about the caste system.

    c. People must marry others from the same caste.

    d. People are divided into five status groups.

3  **In India, _____ determines one's profession or role in society.**

    a. one's race

    b. one's social class

    c. one's level of education

    d. the wealth of one's family

4  **What CANNOT be inferred from the passage?**

    a. Caste systems can be found in various countries.

    b. People can move from one caste to another if they want to.

    c. In caste systems, certain castes are believed to be higher than others.

    d. The Untouchables were not considered a part of India's caste system.

Write the answers in complete sentences.

5  **In India's caste system, which caste did kings and queens belong to?**

_____

6  **Why did people avoid physically touching the Untouchables?**

_____

# SHOW YOUR COMPREHENSION

**Fill in the chart with the phrases from the box.**

The Caste System

| **Characteristics** | • The people in each *varna* have ❶_____ in society. <br> • People are ❷_____ and cannot choose one. |
|---|---|
| **Status Groups** | • Brahmins: ❸_____ <br> • Kshatriyas: soldiers, rulers, and landlords <br> • Vaishyas: ❹_____ <br> • Sudras: ❺_____ <br> • Untouchables: the lowest rank and considered outcasts from society |

certain professions or roles　　merchants and landowning farmers

teachers and priests　　servants and workers　　born into a caste

# SUMMARIZE YOUR READING

**Complete the summary with the words from the box.**

same caste　　by birth　　social status　　interact

the Untouchables　　*varnas*　　occupation　　outcasts

A caste system is a social structure that divides people into groups. Each group has a different ❶_____ and role. In India, one's caste is decided ❷_____ and determines a person's role and ❸_____ in society. In addition, people only ❹_____ or marry others within the ❺_____. India's caste system originally had four main classes, called ❻_____: Brahmins, Kshatriyas, Vaishyas, and Sudras. The lowest rank, ❼_____, was not considered one of the original *varnas*. Members of the Untouchable class were considered ❽_____ from society.

# A New Use for Abandoned Buildings

**WARM UP**

1. What are some reasons people might abandon a building?
2. What items do you recycle in your daily life?

▲ El Ateneo Grand Splendid

## BEFORE YOU READ

**A  Match the words with the definitions below.**

1. _____ abandoned          a. to fail; to break down
2. _____ repurpose          b. left alone; no longer used
3. _____ power plant        c. to make; to produce
4. _____ generate           d. to change into something else
5. _____ transform          e. to find a new use for something
6. _____ collapse           f. a building where electricity is produced

**B  Background Knowledge**

The 19th and early 20th centuries were a productive time in history. Cities were built and then grew larger and larger. Many factories, power plants, and mills were built. However, due to economic problems, many of these buildings were later abandoned as businesses failed and technology changed.

An **abandoned** building can make an area seem depressing and lonely. The structure's walls may become unstable, and the floors may rot. But there is still hope for these old buildings. Some are **repurposed** to preserve the building's history and to give the
5  space a new use. This practice also helps the environment since constructing a new building uses up many resources.

The Tate Modern is a building located in London, England. It was originally a **power plant** built in 1891. During WWII, it became London's only power plant that used oil to **generate** electricity.
10  From 1981, the plant was abandoned for more than ten years. Then, in 1994, a competition was held to redesign the interior into an art gallery. The building reopened in 2000 with millions of people visiting it in the first year alone. Today, it remains one of the world's most popular modern art galleries.

15  Like the Tate Modern, the Zeitz Museum of Contemporary Art Africa was not originally a museum. Built in Cape Town in 1921, the building was first a *grain silo complex until 2001. Later, it was **transformed** into an art museum with the top floors serving as a hotel. The museum opened in 2017 and includes one hundred
20  galleries that display African art.

Across the Atlantic Ocean, El Grand Splendid theater opened in Argentina in 1919. The theater could seat over a thousand people and held a variety of performances. In 1929, the building became a movie theater. Then, Argentina's economy **collapsed**, and the
25  theater closed. It was reopened as a bookstore called El Ateneo Grand Splendid in 2000. Many of the original features remain the same, but the seats were replaced with bookshelves. The bookstore is now considered one of the most beautiful in the world.   **Words 295**

*****grain silo complex** a collection of rounded towers that grains, such as wheat, oats, and soybeans, are stored in

**Q**

**What is the paragraph mainly about?**

P1  Hope for
_____

P2  How a
_____
in London became an art gallery

P3  How a grain silo complex became a (museum / theater)

P4  The different uses of an old (bookstore / theater)

◀ The Zeitz Museum of Contemporary Art Africa

# CHECK YOUR COMPREHENSION

Choose the best answers.

<u>Main idea</u>   1   **What is the main idea of the passage?**

    a. New buildings are of better quality than old ones.

    b. Buildings always get abandoned in hard times.

    c. Old buildings make the best art galleries in the world.

    d. Abandoned buildings can be redesigned and used again.

<u>Details</u>   2   **According to the passage, which is NOT true about the Tate Modern?**

    a. It was first used as a power plant.

    b. It generated electricity in WWII.

    c. It was abandoned until 1981.

    d. It became an art gallery in 2000.

3   **The top floors of the Zeitz Museum of Contemporary Art Africa**

    _____ .

    a. were a power plant

    b. serve as a hotel

    c. are now a bookstore

    d. display African art

4   **Which question CANNOT be answered from paragraph 4?**

    a. When did El Grand Splendid theater open?

    b. What happened to the building in 1929?

    c. Why did El Grand Splendid theater close?

    d. How many people visit El Ateneo Grand Splendid each year?

Write the answers in complete sentences.

5   **How popular is the Tate Modern today?**

    _____

6   **What remains the same and what is different about El Ateneo Grand Splendid?**

    _____

# SHOW YOUR COMPREHENSION

**Fill in the chart with the phrases from the box.**

Recycled Buildings

| | |
|---|---|
| **Tate Modern** | • ❶ _____ built in 1891<br>• abandoned until 1994 when a competition was held to redesign it<br>• reopened in 2000 as an art gallery |
| **Zeitz Museum of Contemporary Art Africa** | • built as a grain silo complex in 1921<br>• abandoned in 2001 and was later ❷ _____<br>• reopened in 2017 and ❸ _____ |
| **El Ateneo Grand Splendid** | • opened as a theater in Argentina in 1919<br>• closed when Argentina's ❹ _____<br>• reopened as ❺ _____ in 2000 |

transformed into an art museum      includes one hundred galleries

originally a power plant      a beautiful bookstore      economy collapsed

# SUMMARIZE YOUR READING

**Complete the summary with the words from the box.**

repurposed      transformed      a bookstore      depressing

originally      abandoned      an art gallery      opened again

Abandoned buildings can make an area feel ❶ _____, but sometimes, they are ❷ _____. The Tate Modern was built in 1891 as a power plant. It was ❸ _____ from 1981 to 1994. At this time, it was redesigned as ❹ _____. Similarly, the Zeitz Museum of Contemporary Art Africa was ❺ _____ a grain silo complex. In 2001, it was abandoned and then later ❻ _____ into an art museum. It ❼ _____ in 2017 and has one hundred galleries inside. Likewise, El Grand Splendid theater was closed after an economic collapse. It was reopened as ❽ _____ in 2000.

# THINK & WRITE 1

**Q** **What Are the Benefits of Recycling?**

**STEP 1** **DISCUSSION** **Talk to your partner and answer the questions.**

1. What materials do you recycle at home?

2. What is one benefit of recycling at home?

**STEP 2** **ORGANIZATION** **Fill in the chart with the phrases from the box.**

| earn a living | keep our air clean |
|---|---|
| creating new jobs | various types of pollution |
| caused by burning garbage | working for recycling centers |

**Introduction**    Recycling benefits the environment in several important ways.

**Body**

Supporting sentence 1: By recycling, we can help reduce

_____.

Details: Recycling lessens the amount of garbage that gets into our water and reduces gas emissions _____.

Supporting sentence 2: Recycling helps save resources.

Details: If we recycle paper and wood, we can preserve trees which help to _____.

Supporting sentence 3: Recycling programs help to create new jobs.

Details: People can _____ by _____.

**Conclusion**    There are many benefits of recycling, including reducing pollution, conserving resources, and _____.

**STEP 3**  `FIRST DRAFT`  **Complete the writing with the phrases from the chart.**

Title What Are the Benefits of Recycling?

Recycling benefits the environment in several important ways.

Firstly, by recycling, we can help reduce _____.
Recycling lessens the amount of garbage that gets into our water and reduces gas emissions _____.

Secondly, recycling helps save resources. If we recycle paper and wood, we can preserve trees which help to _____.

Thirdly, recycling programs help to create new jobs. People can
_____ by _____.

There are many benefits of recycling, including reducing pollution, conserving resources, and _____.

**STEP 4**  `FINAL DRAFT`  **Complete the writing. Replace one of the details with your own idea.**

Title _____

Recycling benefits the environment in several important ways.

Firstly, _____
_____

Secondly, _____
_____

Thirdly, _____
_____

There are many benefits of _____
_____

# CHAPTER
# 02

# UNIT 05 |

**Subject** Earth Science
**Topic** Space Drones

# A Drone on Titan

**WARM UP**

1. What are some ways drones are used?
2. If you could go to space, what planet would you explore?

## BEFORE YOU READ

A **Match the words with the definitions below.**

1. _____ exploration    a. to feel very cold
2. _____ space probe    b. a part of a machine that spins
3. _____ rotor    c. controlled from a distance
4. _____ remotely    d. the parts or substances something is made of
5. _____ composition    e. a robotic spacecraft that explores outer space
6. _____ freeze    f. the act of searching or learning about something

B **Background Knowledge**

Drones are flying vehicles that are usually controlled remotely, meaning they do not need pilots. Drones were originally used for military purposes. However, nowadays drones have many uses. Some of these include photography, filmmaking, farming, mining, and making deliveries. They can even help save people in emergencies.

Saturn has eighty-two moons. Titan, its largest, has captured the attention of many who are interested in space **exploration**. Thanks to **space probe** photographs, scientists now know that Titan has a solid surface of mountains and dunes. Additionally, there are
5 lakes and riverbeds. These important features could help scientists understand how life began on Earth.

**Q**
**What is the paragraph mainly about?**

P1 Saturn's largest (mountains / moon) Titan

To explore other planets, NASA commonly uses rovers, small vehicles that get around on wheels. However, NASA plans to explore Titan using drone technology instead. This special
10 drone, called Dragonfly, is the first of its kind. It is an octocopter, meaning it has eight **rotors**. The drone also has cameras, drills, and other equipment that will collect and study samples. Dragonfly is programmed to guide itself since NASA will not be flying it **remotely**.

P2 The (features / samples) of Dragonfly

15 Dragonfly will travel to Saturn and arrive on Titan in the mid-2030s. Then, it will explore Titan for about two years. NASA intends for the drone to make short flights. During each flight, Dragonfly will collect information about the moon's surface and then send the information back to Earth. Scientists on Earth will study the data
20 and learn all they can about Titan's surface and **composition**.

P3 (How / Where) Dragonfly will operate

Why is Dragonfly such an important step in space exploration? It may not be possible for humans to explore moons like Titan. There is no oxygen there and the temperature is so low that a person would **freeze** to death in seconds. Drones can travel in places that
25 are dangerous for humans. Additionally, the cost of sending a drone is far less than sending a human team. **Words 263**

P4 Why Dragonfly is
_____ in space exploration

# CHECK YOUR COMPREHENSION

Choose the best answers.

Main idea 1 **What is the main idea of the passage?**

    a. Drone technology will improve in the future.

    b. Titan is too dangerous for humans to visit.

    c. A special drone will help scientists explore Titan.

    d. Drones are better at exploring planets than rovers are.

Details 2 **Which is NOT mentioned as a feature of Dragonfly?**

    a. Eight rotors for flying

    b. Self-guided programming

    c. Cameras and drills to collect samples

    d. A radio system to receive data from Earth

3 **Dragonfly will collect information so scientists can learn about the _____ of Titan.**

    a. life

    b. rivers

    c. atmosphere

    d. composition

4 **What CANNOT be inferred from the passage?**

    a. Scientist hope to discover life on Titan's surface.

    b. NASA has not used drones to explore other planets.

    c. Humans would not be able to breathe on Titan.

    d. Dragonfly can survive in Titan's cold temperatures.

Write the answers in complete sentences.

5 **What could Titan's features help scientists understand about Earth?**

_____

6 **According to paragraph 4, why are drones important in space exploration?**

_____

# SHOW YOUR COMPREHENSION

**Fill in the chart with the phrases from the box.**

Dragonfly

| Titan | • the largest of Saturn's 82 moons<br>• has ❶_____, dunes, lakes, and riverbeds |
|---|---|
| **Dragonfly's Features** | • an octocopter ❷_____<br>• has cameras, drills, and ❸_____<br>• programmed to ❹_____ |
| **Dragonfly's Purpose** | • will travel to Saturn and arrive on Titan in the mid-2030s<br>• will ❺_____, collect information, and send it back to Earth |

other equipment to collect samples    with eight rotors

guide itself    make short flights    a solid surface of mountains

# SUMMARIZE YOUR READING

**Complete the summary with the words from the box.**

launch    mid-2030s    dangerous    eight rotors

cost less    study samples    the data    largest moon

Scientists plan to explore Titan, Saturn's ❶_____. NASA will ❷_____
a special drone called Dragonfly. This drone has ❸_____ as well as equipment
that will collect and ❹_____ on Titan. Dragonfly will send ❺_____
back to Earth where scientists will study it. It will help them understand how life on
Earth began. Dragonfly will reach Titan in the ❻_____ and explore the moon
for around two years. It is an important step in space exploration. Drones can travel in
places that are ❼_____ for humans, and they ❽_____ than sending
human teams.

# UNIT 06 |

**Subject** Art & Music
**Topic** Native American Music

# The Songs of the People

**WARM UP**

1. What is music used for in your country?
2. What traditional songs do you know?

## BEFORE YOU READ

**A   Match the words with the definitions below.**

1. _____ nonsense          a. not serious
2. _____ syllable          b. all people of a similar age
3. _____ vocal             c. relating to the human voice
4. _____ light             d. words or sounds that have no meaning
5. _____ generation        e. a part of a word that contains one vowel sound
6. _____ ceremony          f. a formal event for social or religious activities

**B   Background Knowledge**

Native Americans are the people who lived in the United States before Europeans arrived
in the 15th century. With the arrival of Europeans, many Native Americans lost their
land and their lives. There are hundreds of tribes living today, but many are in danger of
disappearing.

Music is an important part of the lives of Native Americans. Most Native Americans consider singing to be the most essential aspect of Native American music. So most songs involve some form of singing. Native Americans sing in their native languages.

5 They also frequently use **nonsense syllables**. Different tribes use different **vocal** techniques. Most also use a wide variety of instruments to make music.

Some of the most common instruments in Native American

10 music are drums. The drums keep the beat of the music, so everyone involved in the performance needs to be able to hear them. Other

15 popular instruments are the *rattle and the flute. There are many different types of rattles and flutes since each tribe has its own way of making them. Accordingly, the sounds they produce depend upon which tribe made them.

20 Men and women also have different roles when it comes to music. Both have their own specific types of music that they sing. For example, men sing songs about going into battle and hunting animals such as bison and deer. On the other hand, women sing songs to their children that are about **lighter** topics.

25 Native Americans use music for many purposes. They pass on their customs and history to new **generations** through their songs. They also use music to speak to their gods in **ceremonies** during which they ask for rain or victory in an upcoming battle. They even have songs that they believe can cure diseases. Simply put, music is of great importance to Native American life.      **Words 255**

*rattle  an object that makes a noise when it is shaken

Q

**What is the paragraph mainly about?**

P1 What Native American (singing / drumming) involves

P2 Common _____ used in Native American music

P3 Musical (roles / styles) for Native American men and women

P4 (Where / How) Native Americans use songs in daily life

# CHECK YOUR COMPREHENSION

Choose the best answers.

<u>Main idea</u>  **1**  **What is the passage mainly about?**

    a. The history of Native American music

    b. The variety of Native American instruments

    c. The characteristics of Native American music

    d. The importance of Native American drumming

<u>Details</u>  **2**  **Which is NOT a feature of Native American music?**

    a. Nonsense syllables

    b. Different vocal techniques

    c. Different gender roles

    d. String instruments

**3**  **According to paragraph 3, which songs are most likely to be sung by men?**

    a. Songs to ensure good health

    b. Songs to bring success in hunting

    c. Songs to help children go to sleep

    d. Songs to help with the growth of crops

**4**  **Which is NOT mentioned as a purpose of Native American music?**

    a. Entertaining leaders

    b. Passing on culture

    c. Talking to gods

    d. Curing illnesses

Write the answers in complete sentences.

**5**  **What is the most essential aspect of Native American music?**

**6**  **Why are the sounds of rattles and flutes different among various Native American tribes?**

# SHOW YOUR COMPREHENSION

**Fill in the chart with the phrases from the box.**

| Native American Music | |
|---|---|
| **Singing** | • Native languages, nonsense syllables, and ❶_____ are used. |
| **Musical Instruments** | • ❷_____ are popular.<br>• Rattles and flutes are made ❸_____. |
| **Gender Roles** | • Men sing ❹_____.<br>• Women sing songs to their children about lighter topics. |
| **Purposes** | • They sing to ❺_____ and history, to communicate with gods, and to cure diseases. |

songs about battles and hunting     differently by different tribes
different vocal techniques     pass on their customs     drums, rattles, and flutes

# SUMMARIZE YOUR READING

**Complete the summary with the words from the box.**

singing     nonsense     ceremonies     role
native languages     musical instruments     traditions     lighter

Music plays an important ❶_____ in Native American life. ❷_____ is the most essential part of Native American music. Native Americans sing in their ❸_____ and frequently use ❹_____ syllables in their songs. Each tribe uses different vocal techniques. They also use various ❺_____ such as drums, rattles, and flutes to make music. When they sing, men usually sing about battles and hunting while women sing about ❻_____ subjects. Native Americans use music to pass on their ❼_____. They also use music in ❽_____ and to cure illnesses.

# What Birth Order Says about You

**WARM UP**

1. How many children are in your family?
2. How would you describe your siblings?

## BEFORE YOU READ

**A** **Match the words with the definitions below.**

1. _____ psychologist    a. relaxed and not easily upset
2. _____ personality    b. someone's character and behavior
3. _____ competitive    c. one thing or aspect that affects something else
4. _____ easygoing    d. needing someone or something for support
5. _____ dependent    e. trying to be more successful than others
6. _____ factor    f. someone who studies the human mind and behavior

**B** **Background Knowledge**

Each person has a unique personality. A personality includes a person's characteristics, attitudes, and abilities. It also includes how a person behaves when alone and with others. According to most psychologists, a person's personality is determined by both biology and the conditions he or she grew up in.

Birth order is the position of a child in a family. For instance, a child might be the oldest, the middle child, the youngest, or an only child. Alfred Adler was a **psychologist** who did research in the early 1900s. He was one of the first theorists to suggest the birth order

5  theory. He believed the birth order of children affects how their **personalities** develop.

For example, the oldest children spend more time with their parents. However, when their younger siblings are born, their parents pay less attention to them. So they try to please their

10  parents to get attention. They are usually responsible and enjoy taking control. Alternatively, middle children tend to be **competitive** since they have to fight their older and younger siblings for their parents' attention. As a result, they sometimes feel left out. Nevertheless, they are frequently more **easygoing** and sociable

15  than their brothers and sisters.

The youngest children are typically more **dependent** on others since they are the babies of their families. They try to get attention from their parents by being charming or funny, so they feel comfortable entertaining others. Lastly, only children—those with

20  no siblings—have personalities similar to those of either oldest or youngest children. Many consider them spoiled and self-centered. Nevertheless, the pressure of being an only child can make them competitive and hardworking.

Not everyone believes the birth order theory is perfect though.

25  **Factors** such as the gender of a child, the age gap between siblings, and the family's culture can affect a child's personality. So can conditions such as the family's income and how parents raise their children. Therefore, people cannot always predict a child's personality according to when he or she was born.   **Words 286**

Q

**What is the paragraph mainly about?**

P1 What the

_____

theory is

P2 The personalities of the (oldest and middle / youngest) children

P3 The personalities of the _____ children

P4 Other conditions that affect

_____

# CHECK YOUR COMPREHENSION

Choose the best answers.

<u>Main idea</u>  **1** **What is the passage mainly about?**

    a. Factors that affect one's personality

    b. The pros and cons of having siblings

    c. How birth order influences one's social skills

    d. The relationship between birth order and personality

<u>Details</u>  **2** **According to the passage, which is true?**

    a. The oldest children enjoy taking on leadership roles.

    b. Middle children are poor at getting along with others.

    c. The youngest children are usually shyer than their siblings.

    d. Only children are usually easygoing and open-minded.

**3** **Which is NOT mentioned as a factor that affects a child's personality?**

    a. Gender

    b. Friends

    c. Family income

    d. The age gap between siblings

**4** **What can be inferred from the passage?**

    a. The birth order theory is considered to be perfect.

    b. Having siblings is better for the development of one's personality.

    c. Birth order is not the only factor that affects one's personality.

    d. Birth order has the most important influence on one's personality.

Write the answers in complete sentences.

**5** **Who suggested the birth order theory?**

_____

**6** **What can make only children competitive and hardworking?**

_____

# SHOW YOUR COMPREHENSION

**Fill in the chart with the phrases from the box.**

| The Birth Order Theory | |
| --- | --- |
| **Birth Order and Personality** | • The oldest children: responsible and ❶ _____ _____ <br> • Middle children: competitive, ❷ _____ <br> • The youngest children: dependent and ❸ _____ _____ <br> • Only children: ❹ _____ |
| **Other Factors** | • Gender, the age gap between siblings, the family's culture and income, and how parents ❺ _____ can affect a child's personality. |

easygoing, and sociable     comfortable entertaining others

competitive and hardworking     raise their children     enjoy taking control

# SUMMARIZE YOUR READING

**Complete the summary with the words from the box.**

age gap     personalities     rely on     hardworking

competitive     culture     responsible     other factors

According to the birth order theory, the order in which children are born influences their ❶ _____ . For example, the oldest children are usually ❷ _____ and like to lead. Middle children tend to be ❸ _____ but are also easygoing and sociable. The youngest children are more likely to ❹ _____ other people, yet they can be entertaining. Only children are often considered spoiled and self-centered, but they are competitive and ❺ _____ . However, the birth order theory is not perfect since ❻ _____ can affect a child's personality. They include gender, the ❼ _____ between siblings, the family's ❽ _____ and income, and how parents raise their children.

# A Great Son of South Africa

**WARM UP**
1. Do you think people should be treated equally?
2. Which world leader do you admire most?

## BEFORE YOU READ

**A Match the words with the definitions below.**

1. _____ chief (*n.*)      a. the state of being in prison
2. _____ sentence (*v.*)   b. the leader of a group
3. _____ imprisonment      c. fighting against someone or something
4. _____ negotiate         d. to punish someone for a crime, usually in a court
5. _____ democratic        e. relating to a political system that values equality
6. _____ resistance        f. to discuss something to reach an agreement

**B Background Knowledge**

Apartheid was a legal system in South Africa in the 1940s. Under this system, Black and white South Africans were forced to live separate lives. This gave white South Africans control over the nation's land, wealth, and government while Black citizens were discriminated against. Apartheid ended in the 1990s with the help of activists like Nelson Mandela.

Nelson Mandela was born on July 18, 1918, in the village of Mvezo in Transkei, South Africa. His father, a tribal **chief**, named him Rolihlahla. It was his school teacher who later gave him the English name Nelson. At the age of nine, his father died, and he was sent to
5 live with the royal family of the Thembu tribe.

In 1944, Mandela joined the *African National Congress (ANC). Through the ANC, he got involved in the Anti-Apartheid Movement. He wanted to free Black South Africans without using violence. However, the government started hurting and killing protestors.
10 This led Mandela to start a military group to fight against the government. He was sent to jail several times until he was finally **sentenced** to life **imprisonment**.

After spending 27 years in prison, Mandela was released by President F.W. de Klerk. Mandela returned as the leader of the ANC
15 and fought for freedom and peace. He also began to **negotiate** with the president to end Apartheid. Finally, Apartheid came to an end, and Mandela began to organize a new **democratic** government. In 1993, Mandela was awarded the Nobel Peace Prize for his work. Then, in 1994, Mandela became the first Black president in South
20 Africa's first fully democratic election.

Mandela was respected and honored not only by the people of South Africa but by people all over the world. Mandela believed
25 in nonviolent **resistance** and continued to spread his ideas to other countries. He worked hard to turn South Africa into a "Rainbow Nation" in which all races are treated and respected equally.
30 On December 5, 2013, the president of South Africa announced Mandela's death. He said, "Our nation has lost its greatest son. Our people have lost a father." Words 288

*__African National Congress (ANC)__ a political party that fought for the rights of African people

Q
**What is the paragraph mainly about?**
[1] Nelson Mandela's (early / late) life

[2] Nelson Mandela's fight against ___

[3] Nelson Mandela's (awards / accomplishments) after prison

[4] The (impact / cause) of Nelson Mandela's life and work

# CHECK YOUR COMPREHENSION

Choose the best answers.

Main idea

**1** **What is the passage mainly about?**

 a. Nelson Mandela's political activities

 b. Nelson Mandela's race to become president

 c. How South Africa became a democratic nation

 d. Nelson Mandela's life and accomplishments

Details

**2** **According to the passage, which is NOT true about Nelson Mandela?**

 a. His original name was Rolihlahla Mandela.

 b. He fought to end Apartheid in South Africa.

 c. His military group fought for the government.

 d. He won an award before becoming president.

**3** **Mandela was imprisoned** _____.

 a. for 27 years

 b. for 30 years

 c. during his youth

 d. for his entire life

**4** **Which is NOT a role Mandela held?**

 a. Tribal chief

 b. Leader of the ANC

 c. President of South Africa

 d. Nobel Peace Prize winner

Write the answers in complete sentences.

**5** **Who gave Mandela the English name Nelson?**

_____

**6** **According to the passage, what is a "Rainbow Nation"?**

_____

# SHOW YOUR COMPREHENSION

**Fill in the chart with the phrases from the box.**

Nelson Mandela

| | |
|---|---|
| **Early Career** | • joined the African National Congress (ANC)<br>• participated in the ① _____<br>• ② _____ to fight against the government |
| **After Imprisonment** | • became the leader of the ANC<br>• negotiated with the president to ③ _____<br>• ④ _____ for his work<br>• was elected ⑤ _____ of South Africa in a fully democratic election |

won the Nobel Peace Prize        the first Black president

Anti-Apartheid Movement        organized a military group        end Apartheid

# SUMMARIZE YOUR READING

**Complete the summary with the words from the box.**

awarded        negotiating        fight against        released

to an end        leader        democratic        imprisonment

Nelson Mandela was born in South Africa in 1918. After joining the ANC, he took part in the Anti-Apartheid Movement. He organized a military group to ① _____ the government and was sentenced to life ② _____. Twenty-seven years later, Mandela was ③ _____ by President F.W. de Klerk. Then, he became the ④ _____ of the ANC and fought for freedom and peace. After ⑤ _____ with the president, he was able to bring Apartheid ⑥ _____ and began to organize a new ⑦ _____ government. In 1993, he was ⑧ _____ the Nobel Peace Prize. A year later, he became the first Black president of South Africa.

# THINK & WRITE 2

**Q** **Who Do You Respect the Most and Why?**

**STEP 1** **DISCUSSION** **Talk to your partner and answer the questions.**

1. Do you know of any people who fought for peace?

2. Who is the person that you respect the most?

**STEP 2** **ORGANIZATION** **Fill in the chart with the phrases from the box.**

| love, compassion, and respect | follow his teachings |
| practices nonviolent resistance | inspires millions of people |
| played an important role politically | is a great political leader |

| | |
|---|---|
| **Introduction** | I respect the Dalai Lama the most for several reasons. |
| **Body** | Supporting sentence 1: The Dalai Lama _____. <br> Details: He has _____ in the fight for Tibetan independence. <br> Supporting sentence 2: He advocates for peaceful solutions for his country. <br> Details: He _____ to Chinese rule. <br> Supporting sentence 3: His voice _____. <br> Details: He gives talks about _____ for others all over the world, and many people _____. |
| **Conclusion** | I respect the Dalai Lama the most because of his great leadership, nonviolent solutions, and spiritual teachings. |

**STEP 3** `FIRST DRAFT` **Complete the writing with the phrases from the chart.**

Title  Who Do You Respect the Most and Why?

I respect the Dalai Lama the most for several reasons.

First of all, the Dalai Lama _____. He has

_____ in the fight for Tibetan independence.

Second, he advocates for peaceful solutions for his country. He

_____ to Chinese rule.

Lastly, his voice _____. He gives talks about

_____ for others all over the world, and many people

_____.

In conclusion, I respect the Dalai Lama the most because of his great

leadership, nonviolent solutions, and spiritual teachings.

**STEP 4** `FINAL DRAFT` **Complete the writing. Replace one of the details with your own idea.**

Title _____

I respect the Dalai Lama the most for several reasons.

First of all, _____

_____

Second, _____

_____

Lastly, _____

_____

In conclusion, I respect the Dalai Lama the most because of _____

_____

# CHAPTER
# 03

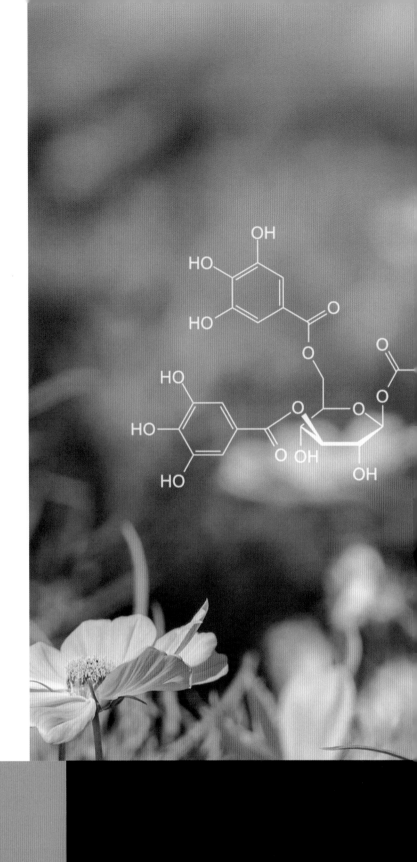

**THINK & WRITE 3**

**How Does Art Positively Affect Our Lives?**

**Subject** Life Science
**Topic** The Platypus

# Mammals That Lay Eggs

**WARM UP**

1. What types of animals usually lay eggs?
2. In your opinion, what is the strangest-looking animal?

## BEFORE YOU READ

**A** **Match the words with the definitions below.**

1. _____ bill
2. _____ burrow
3. _____ carnivorous
4. _____ waddle
5. _____ webbed
6. _____ territory

a. eating only meat
b. the nose and mouth of a duck
c. to walk with short steps
d. having skin that connects the toes together
e. a hole dug by an animal that serves as a home
f. an area of land that an animal considers its own

**B** **Background Knowledge**

Most mammals share a few common features. For example, they often have fur, they give birth to babies, and they produce milk to feed their young. Monotremes are mammals, but they do not give birth. Instead, they lay eggs. The platypus and the echidna are both examples of monotremes.

▲ Echidna

The platypus is one of the most unique-looking animals in the world. Upon seeing one, most people are shocked by the animal's strange appearance. Each platypus has a duck-like **bill**, which is soft and wet and helps the animal find food. Unlike a duck, however, a

5 platypus has thick dark fur and a body that resembles an otter. Most platypus are only about 40-50 cm in length and weigh between 1-1.5 kg.

Platypus are native to eastern Australia. They prefer to make their homes in **burrows** near creeks, rivers, and lakes. Generally,

10 they are **carnivorous**, living off insects, shrimp, and crayfish. Since they keep their eyes and ears closed in the water, they use their bills to feel and locate prey there. Although they tend to **waddle** on the ground, platypus are great swimmers. Their **webbed** front feet help them move efficiently through the water.

15 Platypus are monotremes, which are different from other mammals. This means they raise their young like mammals do, but they don't give birth the same way. Rather, platypus lay eggs like birds do. Additionally, male platypus have a *stinger on each ankle that

20 is full of poison. They use their stingers during mating season to fight other males who enter their **territory**.

Prior to the early 1900s, people hunted

25 platypus freely. Now, the platypus is a protected species, but there are still numerous threats to them. Pollution is making their hunting grounds unusable. In addition, droughts and forest fires are destroying their homes, leaving them without protection or food. Platypus that look for food on land are often killed by *dingoes.

30 However, platypus reserves are helping to preserve this unique species. **Words 276**

***stinger**  a pointed part of an animal or insect that is used to pierce another's skin
***dingo**  a type of wild dog that is native to Australia

---

**Q**

**What is the paragraph mainly about?**

P1 The strange

_____ of the platypus

P2 Where platypus live and how they (make homes / get around)

P3 The (babies / features) of the platypus

P4 _____

to the platypus

# CHECK YOUR COMPREHENSION

Choose the best answers.

Main idea 1 **What is the main idea of the passage?**

    a. The platypus has evolved in order to hunt.

    b. The platypus is a unique animal in Australia.

    c. The platypus has a varied diet of insects and plants.

    d. There are many things that threaten the platypus.

Details 2 **Which does NOT describe a platypus?**

    a. 1-1.5 m in length

    b. Soft, wet duck-like bill

    c. Webbed front feet

    d. Covered in thick dark fur

3 **According to the passage, which is true about the platypus?**

    a. They make their homes in forested areas.

    b. They close their eyes and use their bills to find prey.

    c. They eat plants as well as many insect species.

    d. They give birth to babies as other mammals do.

4 **Which is NOT a current threat to the platypus?**

    a. Pollution is making their hunting grounds dirty.

    b. Their homes are destroyed by fires and droughts.

    c. Dingoes are attacking them when they hunt on land.

    d. Humans are trapping them and keeping them as pets.

Write the answers in complete sentences.

5 **What physical feature helps platypus move in water?**

6 **What do male platypus use their stingers for?**

# SHOW YOUR COMPREHENSION

**Fill in the chart with the phrases from the box.**

The Platypus

| | |
|---|---|
| **Features** | • ❶ _____ and thick dark fur<br>• raise their young like mammals but ❷ _____<br>• males have a stinger that is full of poison |
| **How They Hunt** | • keep ❸ _____ in the water<br>• ❹ _____ to find prey in the water |
| **Threats** | • hunting grounds unusable due to pollution<br>• ❺ _____ leaving them without protection<br>• killed by dingoes when they look for food on land |

lay eggs like birds      droughts and forest fires

use their bills      their eyes and ears closed      duck-like bill

# SUMMARIZE YOUR READING

**Complete the summary with the words from the box.**

carnivorous      poison      many dangers      native

fight off      burrows      their young      locate prey

The platypus is one of the strangest animals in the world. Each platypus has a duck-like bill and thick dark fur. Platypus are ❶ _____ to Australia, preferring to make their ❷ _____ near creeks and rivers. They are ❸ _____ animals and use their bills to ❹ _____ in the water. Platypus are monotremes, which are a type of mammal. Monotremes raise ❺ _____ like other mammals do, but they lay eggs like birds do. Furthermore, males have stingers full of ❻ _____. They use them to ❼ _____ other males during mating season. Platypus are a protected species, but they still face ❽ _____, such as pollution, fires, droughts, and wild dingoes.

# The Trick That Led to Victory

**WARM UP**
1. Which Greek myths have you read?
2. Who are your favorite mythical characters?

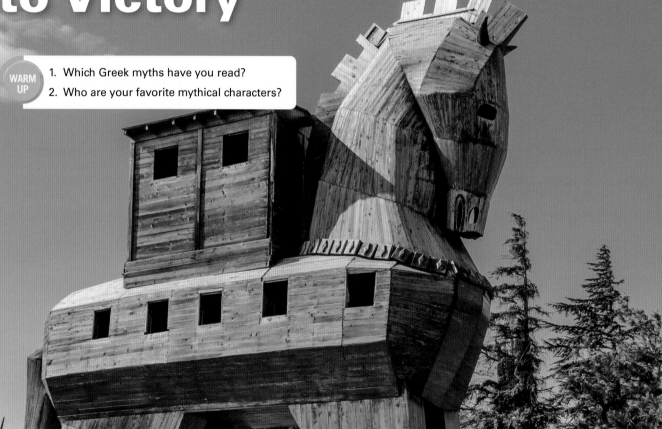

## BEFORE YOU READ

**A   Match the words with the definitions below.**

1. _____ mythological
2. _____ chaos
3. _____ offering
4. _____ assemble
5. _____ set off
6. _____ warrior

a. to begin a journey
b. a gift that is given to please someone
c. a soldier or fighter, especially in the past
d. a state of extreme confusion and disorder
e. based on or related to fictional traditional stories
f. to gather people or things for a particular purpose

**B   Background Knowledge**

The Trojan War is a popular myth about goddesses, royalty, and heroes. However, many historians believe this myth was based on a real war between the Greeks and the Trojans. It likely took place in the 12th century in a city that is now located in modern-day Turkey.

The legend of the Trojan War concerns a **mythological** war between the Greeks and the city of Troy. According to the myth, the Trojan War began at a royal wedding. Eris, the goddess of **chaos**, was not invited to the wedding of Thetis, a goddess of the sea.

5 Offended, Eris stormed into the wedding and threw a golden apple with the words "For the Fairest" inscribed on it.

Aphrodite, Athena, and Hera began to fight over the apple. Then, Zeus sent them to Paris, a Trojan prince, and had him decide who should get the apple. The three goddesses tried to win Paris's vote

10 by making different **offerings**. Paris accepted Aphrodite's offering of the most beautiful woman in the world, Helen.

Even though Helen was already married to Menelaus, the king of Sparta, that did not stop Aphrodite. With Aphrodite's help, Paris took Helen to Troy. Once Menelaus learned that Helen was gone, he

15 asked his brother Agamemnon for help. Agamemnon **assembled** a rescue force and **set off** to Troy. During the war, the Greeks destroyed everything around Troy but could not get past the strong city walls.

20 The war lasted for ten years until Odysseus came up with the idea for the Trojan Horse. Some Greek **warriors** hid inside a giant wooden horse they had built

25 while the rest of the army pretended to leave. The Trojans thought the Greeks had left the horse as a gift, so they took it inside. At night, the Greeks came out of the horse. Then, they opened the gates and let the Greek army

30 inside. They attacked the Trojans by surprise and were finally able to win the war.      Words 277

Q
**What is the paragraph mainly about?**

P1 How the Trojan War (began / ended)

P2 How the goddesses tried to win the _____

P3 Why the Greeks attacked _____

P4 How the (Trojans / Greeks) won the war

# CHECK YOUR COMPREHENSION

Choose the best answers.

Main idea

**1** **What is the passage mainly about?**

　　a. The importance of the Trojan War

　　b. Famous battles in Greek mythology

　　c. Why Odysseus built the Trojan Horse

　　d. How the Trojan War began and ended

Details

**2** **Why did Eris throw a golden apple into the wedding?**

　　a. She threw the apple by mistake.

　　b. She wanted to know who the fairest was.

　　c. She wanted the goddesses to fight with each other.

　　d. She wanted to give the apple to the bride as a wedding gift.

**3** **The Greeks were able to win the Trojan War because** _____.

　　a. they tricked the Trojans

　　b. the Trojans decided to give up

　　c. their army was greater in number

　　d. they were helped by other countries

**4** **Which question CANNOT be answered from the passage?**

　　a. Who was Paris?

　　b. Where did Menelaus rule?

　　c. How long did the Trojan War last?

　　d. What did each goddess offer Paris?

Write the answers in complete sentences.

**5** **What did Agamemnon do to help his brother?**

_____

**6** **What did the Greeks inside the Trojan Horse do at night?**

_____

# SHOW YOUR COMPREHENSION

**Fill in the chart with the phrases from the box.**

The Trojan War

| | |
|---|---|
| **How the Trojan War Begby** | • Eris threw a golden apple inscribed with the words "For the Fairest" into a wedding.<br>• Aphrodite, Athena, and Hera ❶_____.<br>• Paris ❷_____ and was rewarded with Helen.<br>• The Greeks sent a rescue force to Troy to bring Helen back. |
| **How the Greeks Won the War** | • The Greeks built the Trojan Horse to ❸_____.<br>• The Trojans thought ❹_____.<br>• At night, some Greek warriors ❺_____ and let the Greek army inside.<br>• The Greeks attacked the Trojans and won the war. |

chose Aphrodite as the fairest     fought over the apple

trick the Trojans     came out of the horse     the horse was a gift

# SUMMARIZE YOUR READING

**Complete the summary with the words from the box.**

fight over     rescue     fought     married to

golden apple     the fairest     win     mythological

The Trojan War was a ❶_____ war between the Greeks and the city of Troy.
One day, Eris threw a ❷_____ inscribed with the words "For the Fairest" into
a wedding. Then, Aphrodite, Athena, and Hera began to ❸_____ the apple.
Paris chose Aphrodite as ❹_____ after she promised to give him the most
beautiful woman, Helen. Although Helen was ❺_____ the king of Sparta, Paris
took her away to Troy. In response, the Greeks gathered an army to ❻_____
Helen. They ❼_____ for 10 years without a victory. However, by using the
Trojan Horse, the Greeks were able to ❽_____ the war.

# How Do Hostages Feel?

**WARM UP**
1. What would you do in a hostage situation?
2. How do stressful events affect people?

## BEFORE YOU READ

**A  Match the words with the definitions below.**

1. _____ incident
2. _____ hostage
3. _____ bond
4. _____ captor
5. _____ kidnap
6. _____ abuse

a. someone who is kept as a prisoner
b. to take someone away by force
c. an event that does not happen often
d. to treat someone in a cruel and violent way
e. something that unites two or more people
f. someone who keeps another person as a prisoner

**B  Background Knowledge**

People may experience numerous stressful situations in life. At times, these situations can affect a person's physical and mental health. Depending on the type of situation, some people develop mental illnesses. This is especially true when someone experiences a life-threatening event like a car crash, a kidnapping, or a war.

Stockholm Syndrome got its name from an **incident** that happened in Stockholm, Sweden, in 1973. Four people were taken **hostage** in a bank by Jan-Erik Olsson, who had just gotten out of prison. Along with his friend, Clark Olofsson, he held the hostages

5 in the bank for six days. The two criminals threatened to kill the hostages but also showed them some kindness. Six days later, they freed the hostages.

Q
**What is the paragraph mainly about?**

P1 A _____ situation in Stockholm, Sweden

Surprisingly, the hostages did not cooperate with the efforts to rescue them. They even started to think of the police as their

10 enemy. They seemed to have formed an emotional **bond** with the criminals. Even after the rescue, they continued to have these feelings. Swedish doctor Nils Bejerot gave their condition the name Stockholm Syndrome.

P2 How the (doctors / victims) reacted to being hostages

There are certain conditions that cause Stockholm Syndrome.

15 First, the victims feel a great threat to their lives and believe they are going to die. Next, when the **captor** shows the victims some small kindnesses, such as giving them food, the victims start to have positive feelings toward their captor. Then, they start behaving in ways to please their captor. For them, their captor has become

20 the only person who can help them survive.

P3 The _____ that cause Stockholm Syndrome

Stockholm Syndrome does not happen to everyone in a hostage situation. But it often happens to **kidnapped** and **abused** children, battered women, and prisoners of war. In 1991, an 11-year-old girl named Jaycee Dugard was kidnapped and held for 18

25 years. During that time, Dugard bonded with her kidnappers, so she did not try to run away from them.　Words 258

P4 (Who / When) Stockholm Syndrome affects most

# CHECK YOUR COMPREHENSION

Choose the best answers.

Main idea    **1**   **What is the passage mainly about?**

     a. How Stockholm Syndrome got its name

     b. Ways to help someone with Stockholm Syndrome

     c. What Stockholm Syndrome is and how it happens

     d. Who is most likely to suffer from Stockholm Syndrome

Details    **2**   **According to the passage, which is NOT true?**

     a. Clark Olofsson was a friend of Jan-Erik Olsson.

     b. It took six days for the hostages to be rescued.

     c. Stockholm Syndrome was named after a Swedish doctor.

     d. Not all victims in hostage situations experience Stockholm Syndrome.

**3**   **Victims who suffer from Stockholm Syndrome may** _____ .

     a. support and help their captor

     b. try to run away from their captor

     c. feel they will never be rescued

     d. become aggressive toward their captor

**4**   **What kinds of victims are NOT mentioned in the passage?**

     a. Kidnapped children

     b. Abused children

     c. Battered women

     d. Prisoners in jail

Write the answers in complete sentences.

**5**   **What is the first condition that causes Stockholm Syndrome?**

_____

**6**   **Why do some victims try to please their captor?**

_____

# SHOW YOUR COMPREHENSION

**Fill in the chart with the phrases from the box.**

### Stockholm Syndrome

| | |
|---|---|
| **Origin** | • named after a bank robbery in Stockholm, Sweden, in which the hostages ❶_____ with their captors |
| **Conditions** | • First, the victims feel ❷_____.<br>• Next, some small kindnesses ❸_____ toward their captor.<br>• Then, the victims start to act in ways to ❹_____ _____. |
| **People Most Affected** | • ❺_____, battered women, and prisoners of war |

| | | |
|---|---|---|
| kidnapped or abused children | | a great threat to their lives |
| create positive feelings | formed an emotional bond | please their captor |

# SUMMARIZE YOUR READING

**Complete the summary with the words from the box.**

| | | | |
|---|---|---|---|
| hostage | threatened | kindnesses | conditions |
| survive | were rescued | attached to | positive |

Stockholm Syndrome is named after an incident that happened in Stockholm, Sweden. Two criminals held four people ❶_____ in a bank for six days. Although the criminals ❷_____ the hostages with death, the hostages became emotionally ❸_____ the criminals. These feelings continued even after they ❹_____. Certain ❺_____ can cause Stockholm Syndrome to develop. First, the victims feel a threat to their lives. Next, the captor offers some small ❻_____ to the victims. The victims then develop ❼_____ feelings toward their captor. As a result, they try to please their captor because they feel their captor is the only person who can help them ❽_____.

# UNIT 12 |

**Subject** Art & Music
**Topic** Action Painting

# The Art of Splashing

**WARM UP**

1. Do you prefer realistic or abstract art?
2. What is your favorite way to paint?

## BEFORE YOU READ

**A  Match the words with the definitions below.**

1. _____ abstract        a. an explanation
2. _____ impulse         b. to remove; to throw away
3. _____ subconscious    c. not like real things or people
4. _____ convey          d. a sudden strong desire to do something
5. _____ interpretation  e. to express or communicate something
6. _____ get rid of      f. thoughts that you have but are not aware of

## B  Background Knowledge

Abstract Expressionism refers to an art movement in the 1940s and 50s. The style was mostly developed in New York City and spread to other countries. It was the first time an American art movement became famous internationally. The artworks were not realistic-looking. Rather, they were focused on emotions and movement.

Action painting is a form of **abstract** art. It involves the free splashing, spreading, dropping, or throwing of paint onto a canvas. The physical action of painting is itself an important part of the finished work. The paintings focus on the movements of the artists, 5 which express their creative **impulses** and **subconscious**.

Action painting is closely related to Abstract Expressionism, an American art movement in the 1940s. This movement emphasized the creation of art through the human unconscious. Each finished artwork **conveys** the artist's subconscious thoughts. The art is also 10 nonobjective. That is, it does not represent anything in the physical world. This allows the viewers to have their own understanding and **interpretations** of the artwork.

Two important historical events led to action painting in the United States. World War I and World War II left many people feeling 15 shocked by the realities of war. They needed a new kind of art to help them heal and **get rid of** their pain. Action painters helped people express what they wanted to say when they could not find the right words.

20 One of the most influential American action painters was Jackson Pollock. He did not plan how he wanted his paintings to look. 25 Instead, he just let his thoughts and emotions lead him. With the canvas on the floor, he energetically dropped paint onto them. He was famous for his dripping method, which created curving lines and shapes across the canvas. These lines show viewers how he moved his body while painting.     **Words 251**

**Q**

**What is the paragraph mainly about?**

**P1** What (action / splashing) painting involves

**P2** What action painting (removes / conveys)

**P3** The _____ events that affected action painting

**P4** Jackson Pollock and his painting
_____

# CHECK YOUR COMPREHENSION

**Choose the best answers.**

Main idea

1 **What is the passage mainly about?**

    a. The importance of expressing one's feeling

    b. Jackson Pollock's painting style and techniques

    c. The characteristics and history of action painting

    d. The forms of paintings that appeared after World War I and II

Details

2 **An important part of action painting is** _____ .

    a. the energy of the artist

    b. the positioning of the canvas

    c. the way the works are displayed

    d. the movements of the artist

3 **According to the passage, which is true?**

    a. Jackson Pollock carefully planned each of his paintings.

    b. Action painting was influenced by Abstract Expressionism.

    c. Action painters try to describe things as they are in real life.

    d. Action painting does not require the use of a canvas.

4 **Why does the author mention the two world wars?**

    a. To explain why the world wars broke out

    b. To emphasize the bad effects of the wars

    c. To explain how action painting came about

    d. To explain how people can get rid of their pain

**Write the answers in complete sentences.**

5 **If a painting is nonobjective, what does this mean?**

_____

6 **What did Jackson Pollock's dripping technique create?**

_____

# SHOW YOUR COMPREHENSION

Fill in the chart with the phrases from the box.

| Action Painting | |
|---|---|
| **Features** | • focuses on the ❶_____<br>• expresses the artists' ❷_____ |
| **Background** | • closely ❸_____<br>• appeared after World War I and World War II<br>• helped people ❹_____ caused by the two world wars |
| **Jackson Pollock** | • one of the most influential American action painters<br>• famous for his ❺_____ |

related to Abstract Expressionism     physical movements of the artists

creative impulses and subconscious     dripping method     get rid of the pain

# SUMMARIZE YOUR READING

Complete the summary with the words from the box.

subconscious     bodies     influential     splashed

nonobjective     understanding     physical action     world wars

Action painting is a style of art in which the ❶_____ of painting is an important part of the artwork. In action painting, paint is ❷_____ or thrown onto the canvas freely. While painting, the artists focus on the movements of their ❸_____. They let their ❹_____ lead these gestures. The finished artwork is ❺_____, so the viewers can have their own ❻_____ of the paintings. After the two ❼_____, these paintings helped people get rid of the pain caused by the wars. Jackson Pollock was the most ❽_____ artist who used this technique. He was famous for the dripping method that he used to create his art.

# THINK & WRITE 3

**Q** **How Does Art Positively Affect Our Lives?**

**STEP 1** **DISCUSSION** **Talk to your partner and answer the questions.**

1. What forms of art do you know of besides painting?

2. What forms of art do you like the most? Why?

**STEP 2** **ORGANIZATION** **Fill in the chart with the phrases from the box.**

| | |
|---|---|
| drawing, acting | means of communication |
| share them with others | but also provide entertainment |
| help us heal our minds | our psychological problems |

| | |
|---|---|
| **Introduction** | Art affects our lives in many beneficial ways. |
| **Body** | **Supporting sentence 1:** Art is another _____. <br> **Details:** Through art, we can express thoughts and emotions that words cannot describe and _____. <br> **Supporting sentence 2:** Art makes our lives richer. <br> **Details:** For example, beautiful paintings and excellent performances not only make us feel happy _____. <br> **Supporting sentence 3:** Art can _____. <br> **Details:** Art therapies can help us figure out _____ and we can solve them by _____, and doing other activities. |
| **Conclusion** | Art positively affects our daily lives by helping us express our feelings, enjoy our lives, and cure our mental problems. |

**FIRST DRAFT**   **Complete the writing with the phrases from the chart.**

Title  How Does Art Positively Affect Our Lives?

Art affects our lives in many beneficial ways.

First, art is another _____ . Through art, we can express thoughts and emotions that words cannot describe and _____ .

Second, art makes our lives richer. For example, beautiful paintings and excellent performances not only make us feel happy _____ .

Lastly, art can _____ . Art therapies can help us figure out _____ and we can solve them by _____ , and doing other activities.

In conclusion, art positively affects our daily lives by helping us express our feelings, enjoy our lives, and cure our mental problems.

STEP 4   **FINAL DRAFT**   **Complete the writing. Replace one of the details with your own idea.**

Title  _____

Art affects our lives in many beneficial ways.

First, _____

Second, _____

Lastly, _____

In conclusion, art positively affects our daily lives by helping us _____

# Louisa May Alcott

**WARM UP**
1. What is your favorite book and why?
2. How might a war affect an author's writing?

▲ Louisa Alcott's cottage house

## BEFORE YOU READ

**A  Match the words with the definitions below.**

1. _____ prominent     a. good or good enough
2. _____ decent        b. a book that is a part of a set
3. _____ available     c. relating to people's homes
4. _____ domestic      d. important and well-known
5. _____ edit          e. able to be used, bought, or found
6. _____ volume        f. to prepare things for publication

**B  Background Knowledge**

*Little Women* is a popular coming-of-age novel by Louisa May Alcott. It was published in two volumes in the 1860s. The story follows four sisters, Meg, Jo, Beth, and Amy, from childhood into adulthood. The book has been adapted many times for the stage, film, and television. Many generations of fans have enjoyed the story.

Louisa May Alcott was an American novelist. She was born in Germantown, Pennsylvania, on November 29, 1832. She grew up near Boston and Concord, Massachusetts. She was educated by her father and also learned from **prominent** family friends. As a child,
5 she enjoyed writing stories and plays.

Life in the Alcott home was not always easy, however. Louisa's father, an educator and philosopher, was unable to make a **decent** living. From an early age, she began working to support her family. She took any job **available**, but she often worked as a **domestic**
10 servant or a teacher. She also started writing poems and short stories for magazines to earn some money.

When the *Civil War broke out, Louisa wanted to help the *anti-slavery states, so she worked as a nurse at a Union Hospital. She often sent letters home about her experiences. She later **edited**
15 these letters and published them in a book titled *Hospital Sketches*. However, while helping at the hospital, she became ill. She was treated with mercury, but she later suffered from its poisonous effects.

*Hospital Sketches* was the first book
20 Louisa wrote. After that, she wrote a book for girls at the request of her publisher. She wrote about her personal experiences with her three sisters while growing up. This became *Little Women*,
25 her best-known book. It was so successful that a second **volume** was published. A critic said, "The book is the best because it reaches the hearts of those of any age from six to sixty." People also said that it realistically represented daily life at that time.     Words 264

*__Civil War__  the war fought between the northern and southern American states from 1861 to 1865
*__anti-slavery states__  American states that fought to end slavery in the 19th century

**Q**
**What is the paragraph mainly about?**

[P1] Louisa May Alcott's _____ and education

[P2] Louisa May Alcott's (early / late) life difficulties

[P3] Louisa's work during the _____

[P4] Louisa's career as a _____

# CHECK YOUR COMPREHENSION

Choose the best answers.

Main idea    1    **What is the passage mainly about?**

    a. Louisa May Alcott's life and her major works

    b. The characteristics of Louisa May Alcott's novels

    c. How Louisa May Alcott's novels became so famous

    d. The influence of Louisa May Alcott's family on her novels

Details    2    **According to the passage, which is true about Louisa May Alcott?**

    a. She was born in Germany.

    b. She was educated by her sisters.

    c. She started writing as an adult.

    d. She wrote to earn some money.

3    **The novel *Hospital Sketches* was composed of the _____ Louisa wrote.**

    a. diary

    b. poems

    c. letters

    d. stories

4    **What can be inferred from the passage?**

    a. *Hospital Sketches* was Louisa's bestselling book.

    b. *Little Women* was written during the Civil War.

    c. Louisa's novels were not commercially successful.

    d. Louisa's novels were mostly related to her experiences.

Write the answers in complete sentences.

5    **What made Louisa write the novel *Little Women*?**

    _____

6    **Why did a critic say that *Little Women* was the best?**

    _____

# SHOW YOUR COMPREHENSION

**Fill in the chart with the phrases from the box.**

Louisa May Alcott

| | |
|---|---|
| **Early Life** | • educated by her father and famous people around her<br>• enjoyed ❶_____<br>• worked to ❷_____ from an early age |
| **Hospital Sketches** | • her first published book<br>• ❸_____ home during the Civil War |
| **Little Women** | • a book for girls based on her ❹_____<br>• so successful that ❺_____ was published |

experiences with her three sisters    writing stories and plays

a second volume    support her family    based on her letters

# SUMMARIZE YOUR READING

**Complete the summary with the words from the box.**

learned a lot    represented    a nurse    realistically

her experiences    early age    her father    novelist

Louisa May Alcott, an American ❶_____, is well known for her book *Little Women*. She grew up in a poor family, but she ❷_____ from ❸_____ and the great people around her. To support her family, she began working from a(n) ❹_____. During the Civil War, she worked as ❺_____ at a Union Hospital. The letters she wrote about ❻_____ at the hospital were published in her book *Hospital Sketches*. In her famous book *Little Women*, she wrote stories about her life with her three sisters. The book is considered to be one of the best because it ❼_____ daily life during that time ❽_____.

# UNIT 14 |

**Subject** Language
**Topic** Mythology

# The Story of Winter

**WARM UP**

1. When does winter begin and end in your country?
2. Do you know of any myths about winter?

## BEFORE YOU READ

**A   Match the words with the definitions below.**

1. _____ fertility
2. _____ miserable
3. _____ destruction
4. _____ obey
5. _____ trick
6. _____ compromise

a. extremely unhappy
b. the state of being destroyed
c. to do what someone tells you to do
d. the ability of the soil to produce good crops
e. an agreement in order to end an argument
f. to make someone believe something that is not true

**B   Background Knowledge**

Over time, Greek myths were adopted by other cultures. The myths were translated into different languages, and the stories were changed. Thus, there are now various versions of certain myths. The Persephone myth is one such example. In some versions, Persephone was a victim. In others, she was the powerful Queen of the Underworld.

In Greek mythology, the story of Persephone explains why there are different seasons. According to the story, a long time ago, there was just one season. Year after year, people enjoyed warm weather and good harvests. This was thanks to the goddess of the harvest
5 and **fertility**, Demeter.

Persephone was the daughter of Demeter and Zeus. One day, when Persephone was picking flowers outside, Hades, the god of the underworld, suddenly appeared and dragged her to the underworld. He had been hit by one of Eros's arrows and lost his
10 heart to Persephone. Demeter could not find her daughter and became **miserable**. She refused to give up her search, but her sadness spread and caused the **destruction** of crops and livestock.

Zeus realized this was a big problem and sent Hermes, the messenger god, to Hades to tell him to let Persephone go. Hades
15 had no choice but to **obey** Zeus. Before sending Persephone away, Hades **tricked** her into eating some pomegranate seeds. He knew that if someone ate something while in the underworld, he or she had to stay forever. Persephone and Demeter finally reunited, but when Zeus asked Persephone if she
20 had eaten anything, she mentioned the pomegranate seeds.

Zeus helped Demeter and Hades reach a **compromise**. Persephone would spend four months in the underworld and the rest of
25 the year with her mother. However, Demeter loved her daughter so much that when she was gone, the land became cold and infertile. Then, when Persephone returned, plants flowered again to welcome her. People
30 believe that when Persephone leaves her mother, it becomes winter. When she returns home, spring begins. **Words 271**

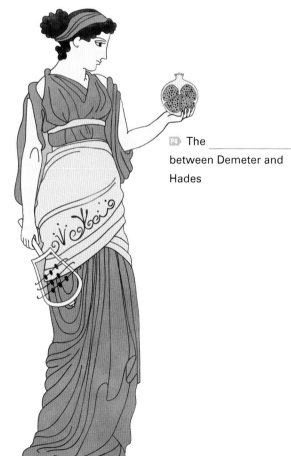

**What is the paragraph mainly about?**

▶ What the story of Persephone (explains / predicts)

▶ Why _____ became miserable and put the land in danger

▶ How Persephone returned to (the underworld / her mother)

▶ The _____ between Demeter and Hades

# CHECK YOUR COMPREHENSION

Choose the best answers.

<u>Main idea</u>  1  **What is the passage mainly about?**

  a.  Hades' love for Persephone

  b.  The reason we have four seasons

  c.  Demeter's sadness over her lost daughter

  d.  A Greek myth about winter and spring

<u>Details</u>  2  **According to the passage, which is NOT true about Demeter?**

  a.  She is the mother of Persephone.

  b.  She makes crops grow on the Earth.

  c.  She sent Hermes to bring Persephone back.

  d.  She caused winter when she became sad.

3  **Persephone must return to the underworld because** _____.

  a.  she loves Hades so much

  b.  the Earth is too cold in winter

  c.  she can meet her mother there

  d.  she ate some pomegranate seeds

4  **What happens when Persephone returns to the underworld?**

  a.  The land turns cold.

  b.  Flowers start growing again.

  c.  People have a good harvest.

  d.  Persephone reunites with her mother.

Write the answers in complete sentences.

5  **What did Demeter's sadness cause when she was looking for Persephone?**

_____

6  **What compromise did Demeter and Hades make?**

_____

# SHOW YOUR COMPREHENSION

**Fill in the chart with the phrases from the box.**

The Persephone Myth

| | |
|---|---|
| **The Kidnapping of Persephone** | • One day, Hades took Persephone ❶_____. <br> • Zeus sent Hermes to ❷_____. <br> • Before ❸_____, she ate some pomegranate seeds. |
| **The Compromise Between Demeter and Hades** | • Persephone would spend four months in the underworld and the other months ❹_____. <br> • When she leaves her mother, ❺_____. <br> • When she returns home, spring begins. |

to the underworld     Persephone was released

bring Persephone back     it becomes winter     with her mother

# SUMMARIZE YOUR READING

**Complete the summary with the words from the box.**

in love     release     tricked     plants flowered

the harvest     infertile     four months     stop growing

Demeter, the goddess of ❶_____, had a daughter named Persephone. One day, Hades fell ❷_____ with Persephone and took her to the underworld. Demeter became so sad that she caused crops to ❸_____. Zeus eventually ordered Hades to ❹_____ Persephone. Before sending her away, Hades ❺_____ Persephone into eating some pomegranate seeds. This meant that she had to stay in the underworld forever. Zeus made a deal in which Persephone would spend ❻_____ in the underworld and the other months with her mother. However, when Persephone was gone, the land became cold and ❼_____. When she returned, ❽_____ and spring began again.

# An Artistic Life

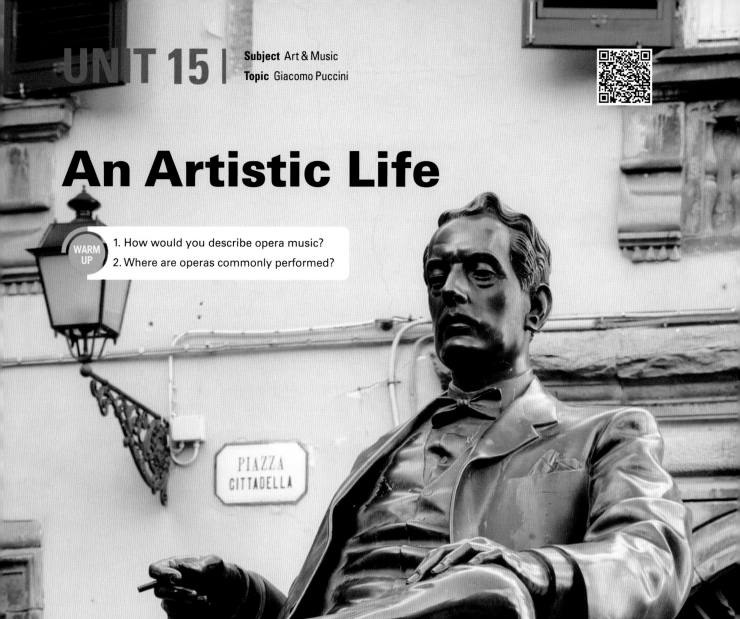

**WARM UP**

1. How would you describe opera music?
2. Where are operas commonly performed?

PIAZZA CITTADELLA

## BEFORE YOU READ

**A   Match the words with the definitions below.**

1. _____ composer       a. the words of a song
2. _____ plot           b. someone who writes music
3. _____ lyrics         c. to place one's feelings or ideas on something
4. _____ project (v.)   d. to find out what illness someone has
5. _____ diagnose       e. a series of events that make up a story
6. _____ complication   f. a medical problem that happens while someone is already ill

**B   Background Knowledge**

Opera is a type of theater that includes both singing as well as orchestra music. Operas are commonly divided into acts. Some operas have between two and five acts. However, some have only one. Each act contains a different type of performance. The characters might sing alone or with other characters.

Giacomo Puccini was born in Lucca, Italy, in 1858. He came from a long line of passionate musicians. However, it was not until he saw a performance of Verdi's *Aida* that he decided to become an opera **composer**. For this reason, he went to study at the Milan
5  Conservatory. He then entered a one-act opera competition and wrote his first opera, *Le Villi*.

Among Puccini's greatest works are *La Boheme*, *Tosca*, *Madama*
10  *Butterfly*, and *Turandot*. *La Boheme* became popular very quickly and was performed all around the world. His

◀ Turandot

15  next work was *Tosca*, which is known for its well-organized **plot** and beautiful **lyrics**. *Madama Butterfly* had a rough start, but after some reworking, it became another of his most successful operas. *Turandot* was his last opera, but he died before completing it.

During Puccini's career, it was said that he was always in love
20  with a new woman whenever he wrote a new opera. It was also said that he would **project** images of the women he loved onto his works. For instance, the heroine in *The Girl of Golden West* was based on one of his lovers. But who the actual person was remains an unsolved mystery.

25  Puccini's success gave him not only fame but also a lot of money. He used it on what he enjoyed the most: fine cigars. However, he began suffering from constant sore throats and was later **diagnosed** with throat cancer. He went to Brussels to receive some experimental treatments. Unfortunately, during surgery, there
30  were some **complications**, which led to him having a heart attack. Puccini died in Brussels in 1924.  Words 267

Q

**What is the paragraph mainly about?**

P1 ▶ Giacomo Puccini's interest in (operas / education)

P2 ▶ Operas (performed / composed) by Puccini

P3 ▶ The (location / inspiration) behind Puccini's operas

P4 ▶ How Puccini became sick and

# CHECK YOUR COMPREHENSION

Choose the best answers.

**1** **What is the passage mainly about?**

    a. Famous operas of the 19th century

    b. The life and work of Giacomo Puccini

    c. Giacomo Puccini's real-life love story

    d. Giacomo Puccini's most famous opera

**2** **According to the passage, which is NOT true?**

    a. Puccini came from a musical family.

    b. Puccini included his love life in his works.

    c. Puccini's love of cigars led to his death.

    d. Puccini became famous after his death.

**3** **One of Puccini's famous operas, *Turandot*, was _____.**

    a. his first opera

    b. based on his life

    c. left unfinished by him

    d. the world's most performed opera

**4** **Which question CANNOT be answered from the passage?**

    a. When was Puccini born?

    b. Where did Puccini go to school?

    c. What are some of Puccini's famous works?

    d. How many of Puccini's works were based on his lovers?

Write the answers in complete sentences.

**5** **Why did Puccini decide to become an opera composer?**

_____

**6** **Why did Puccini go to Brussels?**

_____

# SHOW YOUR COMPREHENSION

**Fill in the chart with the phrases from the box.**

Giacomo Puccini

| | |
|---|---|
| **Early Life** | • decided to ❶_____ after seeing Verdi's *Aida* |
| **His Works** | • *La Boheme*: ❷_____<br>• *Tosca*: known for its well-organized plot and beautiful lyrics<br>• *Madama Butterfly*: had a rough start but was successful<br>• *Turandot*: his last opera, ❸_____<br>• *The Girl of Golden West*: based on ❹_____ |
| **Illness and Death** | • ❺_____ and died in 1924 |

become an opera composer    diagnosed with throat cancer

one of his lovers    left incomplete    became popular very quickly

# SUMMARIZE YOUR READING

**Complete the summary with the words from the box.**

*Aida*    became ill    his works    born into

women    well-known    complications    own time

Giacomo Puccini was ❶_____ a musical family in Italy in 1858. He decided to become an opera composer after seeing Verdi's opera ❷_____, so he went to study music at the Milan Conservatory. Aside from his first opera *Le Villi,* he also wrote *La Boheme, Tosca, Madama Butterfly*, and *Turandot*, which are all ❸_____ operas today. His success made him quite famous in his ❹_____ as well. It is believed that Puccini fell in love with many ❺_____ in his lifetime, and he often included these women in ❻_____. Puccini ❼_____ with throat cancer and eventually died in 1924 after ❽_____ during surgery.

# A Satirical Awards Ceremony

**WARM UP**

1. Have you ever won an award? What was the award for?

2. In your opinion, what is the most useful invention?

## BEFORE YOU READ

**A Match the words with the definitions below.**

1. _____ recognize    a. to have good effects

2. _____ counterpart    b. to give, often an award

3. _____ satirical    c. criticizing something in a funny way

4. _____ present    d. a device that catches a living thing

5. _____ benefit (*v.*)    e. to give public attention to someone for an achievement

6. _____ trap    f. a person or thing that has the same purpose as another

## B Background Knowledge

The Nobel Prize is a famous award founded by Alfred Nobel over 100 years ago. The prize rewards great work in various fields, such as physics, chemistry, medicine, literature, etc. Nationality doesn't matter; anyone around the world can receive the award which includes a gold medal, a diploma, and a cash prize.

The Nobel Prize is a well-known award that **recognizes** achievements in various subjects. People who receive a Nobel Prize feel it's a great honor. However, some receive the Ig Nobel Prize instead. Unlike its **counterpart**, the Ig Nobel Prize is a **satirical**

5 award. It does not recognize serious achievements. Rather, it honors research that makes people laugh first and then think.

The Ig Nobel Prize was founded in 1991 by a humorous science magazine. Ten prizes are awarded each year in several categories, such as physics, chemistry, literature, and more. The prizes are

10 often **presented** by actual Nobel Prize winners. The ceremony is considered a fun and humorous event. For example, it is tradition for the attendees to throw paper airplanes onto the stage during the ceremony.

Most Ig Nobel Prizes recognize research that seems comical

15 in some way. For instance, in 2000, Sir Andre Geim received an award for making a frog float in the air using magnetism. An award was also given to the researchers of the "five-second rule." This rule states that food on the floor is still safe to eat if less than five seconds has passed. Such research is considered humorous

20 because it doesn't **benefit** humanity in any way.

On the other hand, what may seem trivial might actually have great benefits. A 2006 study, for example, examined the way malaria-carrying mosquitoes were attracted to smells. It determined that these mosquitoes preferred the

25 smells of cheese and human feet. This research helped scientists create special mosquito **traps**. The traps use smells to capture mosquitoes. They have helped some African nations prevent the spread

30 of malaria. Although the research seemed funny at first, it went on to help many people.

Words 284

Q

**What is the paragraph mainly about?**

[P1] The difference between the Nobel Prize and the

_____

[P2] How the Ig Nobel Prizes are (researched / awarded) each year

[P3] What type of

_____ the Ig Nobel Prize recognizes

[P4] The potential (benefits / disadvantages) of trivial research

# CHECK YOUR COMPREHENSION

Choose the best answers.

**Main idea**

**1** **What is the main idea of the passage?**

　　a. Ig Nobel Prize winners go on to win a real Nobel Prize later in life.

　　b. The Ig Nobel Prize has become more popular than the Nobel Prize.

　　c. The Ig Nobel Prize focuses on research that does not benefit humanity.

　　d. The Ig Nobel Prize celebrates research that makes people laugh and then think.

**Details**

**2** **According to the passage, which is NOT true about the Ig Nobel Prize?**

　　a. The ceremony is held annually.

　　b. It was founded by a humorous magazine.

　　c. Nobel Prize winners often award the prizes.

　　d. Awards are presented in three subject areas.

**3** _____ is a tradition that happens during the Ig Nobel Prize ceremony.

　　a. Refusing awards

　　b. Receiving a cash prize

　　c. Standing up and clapping

　　d. Throwing paper airplanes

**4** **Which question CANNOT be answered from the passage?**

　　a. Where are the Ig Nobel Prize awards held?

　　b. What did Sir Andre Geim receive an award for?

　　c. What type of research does the Ig Nobel Prize honor?

　　d. How is the Ig Nobel Prize different from the original?

Write the answers in complete sentences.

**5** **What does the "five-second rule" state?**

_____

**6** **How have the mosquito traps helped some African nations?**

_____

# SHOW YOUR COMPREHENSION

**Fill in the chart with the phrases from the box.**

The Ig Nobel Prize

| What It Is | • founded in 1991 by ❶_____<br>• considered ❷_____ |
|---|---|
| Winners | • research that ❸_____ in some way<br>• Sir Andre Geim – won for making a frog float<br>• researchers of the "five-second rule" also won |
| Trivial Research That Has Benefits | • a study determined ❹_____ to the smells of cheese and feet<br>• special traps that use smells were created<br>• helped some African nations ❺_____ |

prevent the spread of malaria    a humorous science magazine

a fun and humorous event    seems comical    mosquitoes were attracted

# SUMMARIZE YOUR READING

**Complete the summary with the words from the box.**

determined    ten prizes    satirical    prevent

great benefits    float    think    serious research

Unlike the Nobel Prize, the Ig Nobel Prize does not recognize ❶_____.
Rather, it is a ❷_____ award that honors research that makes people laugh
before making them ❸_____. The Ig Nobel Prize was founded in 1991 with
❹_____ awarded each year. Winners include Sir Andre Geim, who made a
frog ❺_____ using magnetism, and the researchers of the "five-second rule."
Sometimes, however, what seems like trivial research also has ❻_____ for
humanity. A 2006 study, for example, ❼_____ that mosquitoes love the smells
of cheese and feet. The research was used to make mosquito traps. These traps have
helped ❽_____ the spread of malaria in some African countries.

# THINK & WRITE 4

**What Is the Greatest Invention in the World?**

**STEP 1** `DISCUSSION` **Talk to your partner and answer the questions.**

1. What invention do you use almost every day?

2. What do you usually use the invention for?

**STEP 2** `ORGANIZATION` **Fill in the chart with the phrases from the box.**

| | |
|---|---|
| order many products online | watch movies and TV programs |
| contact each other easily | gives people easy access to |
| makes shopping easy | connects people all around the world |

| | |
|---|---|
| **Introduction** | I believe the greatest invention in the world is the Internet. |
| **Body** | **Supporting sentence 1:** The Internet _____. <br> **Details:** Through email and social networking services, people can _____ despite long distances. <br> **Supporting sentence 2:** The Internet also _____. <br> **Details:** You can _____. They are often cheaper than at stores, and they will be delivered to you. <br> **Supporting sentence 3:** The Internet _____ entertainment and information. <br> **Details:** You can _____ anytime. Also, you can stay up to date on the news. |
| **Conclusion** | The Internet is very useful because we can stay connected to the world, buy things easily, and access entertainment and information. |

**FIRST DRAFT** **Complete the writing with the phrases from the chart.**

Title What Is the Greatest Invention in the World?

I believe the greatest invention in the world is the Internet.

First, the Internet _____. Through email and social networking services, people can _____ despite long distances.

Second, the Internet also _____. You can _____ _____. They are often cheaper than at stores, and they will be delivered to you.

Lastly, the Internet _____ entertainment and information. You can _____ anytime. Also, you can stay up to date on the news.

In short, the Internet is very useful because we can stay connected to the world, buy things easily, and access entertainment and information.

STEP 4 **FINAL DRAFT** **Complete the writing. Replace one of the details with your own idea.**

Title _____

I believe the greatest invention in the world is the Internet.

First, _____

_____

Second, _____

_____

Lastly, _____

_____

In short, the Internet is very useful because we can _____

# CHAPTER
## 05

**THINK & WRITE 5**

**What Treasures Help Us Understand the Past Better?**

# UNIT 17 |

**Subject** History
**Topic** The Big Lie

# That Sounds Too Strange to Be False

**WARM UP**

1. Have you ever lied to a friend? Why?
2. What sort of lies are easy to believe?

## BEFORE YOU READ

### A Match the words with the definitions below.

| | | | |
|---|---|---|---|
| 1. _____ | false | a. | unlikely to be true |
| 2. _____ | statement | b. | incorrect or untrue |
| 3. _____ | convince | c. | a fact that is accepted as true |
| 4. _____ | truth | d. | something said, often given as fact |
| 5. _____ | unbelievable | e. | to make someone believe something is true |
| 6. _____ | prove | f. | to show that something is true by using evidence |

### B Background Knowledge

World War II lasted from 1939 to 1945. During the war, Nazi Germany put millions of European Jewish people into prison camps. Many lived in terrible conditions in the camps, and around 6 million were murdered. The Holocaust is remembered as one of the most tragic events in history.

The "big lie" is a technique used to spread a **false** idea. Adolf Hitler was one of the first people to use and create the expression "big lie." He explained it in his book *Mein Kampf*. The goal of anyone telling a big lie is to influence how people feel or what they
5  think about something. The big lie is repeated again and again. Sooner or later, people come to believe that the big lie is true no matter how shocking it may be.

Hitler's big lie was the idea
10 that Jewish people were the real enemies of Germany. He also said that they were the ones responsible for Germany losing World War I. At the time, Jewish people already experienced
15 discrimination. Hitler worsened this discrimination by making numerous false **statements** about them. Eventually, he was able to **convince** many non-Jewish Germans that his lies were the **truth**.

Why did Hitler's big lie work so effectively? It is common for most people to tell small lies. Others can easily recognize that
20 these small lies are not the truth. However, when a person says something **unbelievable**, it is hard for others to imagine someone telling such a huge lie. Many people accepted Hitler's big lie for this reason.

Many big lies have been told throughout history and are still
25 told today. The technique has been **proven** to be one of the best ways to control the minds of others. These days, rumors about celebrities are common even though they are mostly untrue. At first, these rumors are difficult to believe, but in the end, many people think they are true.   Words 269

Q

**What is the paragraph mainly about?**

P1 What the big lie _____ is

P2 The big lie that _____ told

P3 How big lies (start / work)

P4 How (big / small) lies are used today

# CHECK YOUR COMPREHENSION

Choose the best answers.

**Main idea**    **1**    **What is the passage mainly about?**

a. How big lies work

b. Big lies about celebrities

c. Why the Germans lost World War I

d. Discrimination against Jewish people in Germany

**Details**    **2**    **According to the passage, which is NOT true?**

a. Big lies are told frequently.

b. Only Hitler used the term big lie.

c. Big lies may change people's views on something.

d. Hitler spread false information about Jewish people.

**3**    **The big lie technique was used to make _____ believe that Jewish people were the cause of Germany's loss in World War I.**

a. Hitler

b. celebrities

c. most Germans

d. Jewish people

**4**    **What can be inferred from the passage?**

a. People often find it difficult to tell small lies.

b. Most people prefer to tell big lies over small lies.

c. Jewish people caused Germany to lose World War I.

d. Not all of the rumors about celebrities are true.

Write the answers in complete sentences.

**5**    **What is the goal of anyone telling a big lie?**

_____

**6**    **Why do people believe unbelievable lies?**

_____

# SHOW YOUR COMPREHENSION

**Fill in the chart with the phrases from the box.**

| | The Big Lie Technique |
|---|---|
| **Goal** | • to influence how ❶_____ about something |
| **How It Works** | • A big lie is often ❷_____ .<br>• People do not expect someone to ❸_____ .<br>• Eventually, people accept the lie as the truth. |
| **Example** | • Hitler said that Germany had lost World War I<br>  ❹_____ .<br>• Many Germans began to believe Jewish people were<br>  ❺_____ . |

because of Jewish people      people feel or think
repeated to people      their real enemies      tell such a huge lie

# SUMMARIZE YOUR READING

**Complete the summary with the words from the box.**

true      small lies      frequently      control
unbelievable      responsible      common      big lie

The big lie technique is the idea that if a lie is big enough and is told ❶_____ ,
people tend to believe it. People often don't believe ❷_____ because they
are ❸_____ and easy to recognize. However, it is hard for them to accept that
someone would tell a(n) ❹_____ lie. Thus, it is easier to believe the lie is
❺_____ . Hitler used the ❻_____ technique on the German people.
He wanted Germans to believe that Jewish people were ❼_____ for Germany's
defeat in World War I. To this day, big lies are told as a way to ❽_____ the
minds of others.

# UNIT 18 |

**Subject** Life Science
**Topic** Vitamin D

# Why Do We Need Vitamin D?

**WARM UP**

1. How do you make sure you get enough vitamins?

2. What might happen if you don't get enough vitamins?

## BEFORE YOU READ

**A  Match the words with the definitions below.**

1. _____ nervous system
2. _____ exposure
3. _____ supplement
4. _____ deficiency
5. _____ overdo
6. _____ digestive

a. to do too much; to take too much

b. the brain and all the nerves in the body

c. the state of not having enough of something

d. something that is added; something extra

e. relating to the body's way of eating and using food

f. the state of being affected by something; being shown something

**B  Background Knowledge**

There are thirteen vitamins that are necessary for good health. When taken in proper amounts, vitamins help the body in numerous ways. For example, some vitamins make bones stronger. Others heal wounds and help the body fight diseases. Some even help the body change food into energy.

Like all vitamins, vitamin D is important for good health. Vitamin D has many benefits that improve bone health as well as your muscles, **nervous system**, and immune system. There are three main ways to get vitamin D into your body. The first is through the
5 skin via **exposure** to sunlight. The other two are by consuming it in the form of food or **supplements**.

A lack of vitamin D can be a serious health problem. For example, vitamin D **deficiency** can affect bone density. A loss of bone might mean brittle bones as a person ages. Brittle bones
10 often break very easily. In addition to weak bones, vitamin D deficiency may cause bone pain and weak muscles. There may also be a connection between vitamin D deficiency and diabetes, cancer, and *autoimmune diseases.

The amount of vitamin D a person needs per day depends on
15 age. Babies and children tend to need less vitamin D than adults do. Adults over the age of 71 need the most in order to stay in good health. To ensure you get enough vitamin D, consume foods like fatty fish, cheese, mushrooms, and eggs. Multivitamins also include an adequate amount of vitamin D.

20 But don't **overdo** it as vitamin D can also cause health problems. Too much vitamin D can lead to **digestive** issues like nausea and vomiting. It might also damage the kidneys or lead to too much calcium in the blood. An excess of calcium in the blood can cause confusion and dizziness. Having too much vitamin D is usually not
25 caused by food intake or sun exposure. Rather, it's the result of taking too many supplements.　**Words 276**

*autoimmune disease  an illness in which the immune system attacks part of the body by mistake

Q

**What is the paragraph mainly about?**

🔲 Vitamin D's relationship to the (body / sun)

🔲 The effects of vitamin D (intake / deficiency)

🔲 How much vitamin D is needed for

_____

🔲 The effects of

_____

vitamin D

# CHECK YOUR COMPREHENSION

Choose the best answers.

<u>Main idea</u>    1    **What is the main idea of the passage?**

a.  The best way to get enough vitamin D is through sun exposure.

b.  Having too much vitamin D in your body can lead to an early death.

c.  A well-balanced diet can give a person enough vitamins and minerals.

d.  It is important to get the correct amount of vitamin D to stay healthy.

<u>Details</u>    2    **According to the passage, what might vitamin D deficiency cause?**

a.  Confusion and dizziness

b.  Nausea and vomiting

c.  Brittle bones and weak muscles

d.  Poor vision and kidney problems

3    _____ **require the most vitamin D to stay healthy.**

a.  Babies and children

b.  Teenagers

c.  Adults under 50

d.  Adults over 71

4    **Why does the author mention fatty fish, cheese, mushrooms, and eggs?**

a.  To recommend foods that are high in vitamin D

b.  To explain when to start taking multivitamins

c.  To warn against consuming too much vitamin D

d.  To list foods that prevent too much sun exposure

Write the answers in complete sentences.

5    **What diseases are vitamin D deficiency possibly connected to?**

_____

6    **What is the cause of too much Vitamin D in the body?**

_____

# SHOW YOUR COMPREHENSION

**Fill in the chart with the phrases from the box.**

| | Vitamin D |
|---|---|
| **Vitamin D Deficiency** | • can affect bone density<br>• can also ❶_____ and weak muscles<br>• may be connected to diabetes, ❷_____ |
| **How Much Is Needed** | • babies and ❸_____ than adults do<br>• adults over 71 ❹_____ |
| **Too Much Vitamin D** | • can lead to digestive issues<br>• might damage the kidneys or ❺_____ in the blood |

lead to too much calcium      cancer, and autoimmune diseases

cause bone pain      children need less      need the most

# SUMMARIZE YOUR READING

**Complete the summary with the words from the box.**

immune system      too much      improve      supplements

digestive      enough      weak muscles      sun exposure

Vitamin D can ❶_____ your bone health as well as your muscles, nervous system, and ❷_____. You get vitamin D through ❸_____ or by consuming it in the form of food and ❹_____. Vitamin D deficiency is a serious problem that can cause bone loss and ❺_____. It may also be connected to more serious problems like diabetes, cancer, and autoimmune diseases. It is important to get ❻_____ vitamin D. Children need less than adults, and adults over age 71 need the most. But ❼_____ vitamin D can also cause health problems. ❽_____ issues, kidney damage, and too much calcium in the blood are just a few examples.

# Selling a House to Buy Tulips

**WARM UP**

1. What is your most expensive item? Is it worth the price?
2. What product do you think is overpriced?

## BEFORE YOU READ

**A**  **Match the words with the definitions below.**

1. _____ goods
2. _____ consumer
3. _____ stabilize
4. _____ bulb
5. _____ speculator
6. _____ suspect (v.)

a. things that are made to be sold
b. to make something steady or unchanging
c. to think that something is probably true
d. someone who buys things or pays for services
e. a root shaped like a ball that grows into a flower
f. someone who buys things to sell them again at higher prices

**B**  **Background Knowledge**

Although tulips are popular all over the world, they originally came from Central Asia. Later, they were grown in what is now present-day Turkey. Tulips were brought to Western Europe in the 1500s. Europeans were fascinated by these rare and exotic-looking flowers. Tulips became especially popular in the Netherlands in the 1600s.

The law of supply and demand explains how the prices of goods and services are determined. Supply means the amount of **goods** and services that can be produced. Demand is the amount of goods and services that **consumers** want to buy. Prices rise when there is

5 an increase in demand. When there is an increase in supply, prices go down.

When the amount of goods in demand is the same as the amount of goods being supplied, it **stabilizes** prices. However, if either side increases too much, it can create economic problems.

10 Tulip Mania was an example of this. It happened in the Netherlands in the 1630s. At the time, the demand for tulip **bulbs** rose so rapidly that prices went out of control. Then, prices dropped suddenly.

After tulips were introduced to the Netherlands, they became a symbol of high status among the wealthy class. As a result, rare

15 varieties were seen as valuable and luxurious items and were traded at high prices. Once they gained popularity as a trading product, traders and **speculators** bought them to make large profits. Even ordinary people started to believe trading tulips was an easy way to make money.

20 As more people became interested in tulip bulbs, prices rose even more. Some people began selling all of their possessions in order to buy them. The situation created an economic bubble in which prices became

25 unbelievably higher than the value of the actual items. As the supply increased, however, some people **suspected** the demand for tulips would not last and began to sell their tulips. Eventually, prices dropped, and many were left poor with a supply of tulips that were worthless.

Words 277

Q

**What is the paragraph mainly about?**

1 How supply and

_____

works

2 What Tulip

_____

was

3 How Tulip Mania
(began / ended)

4 How tulips
eventually became
(worthless / expensive)

# CHECK YOUR COMPREHENSION

Choose the best answers.

Main idea 1  **What is the passage mainly about?**

    a. The history of tulips in the Netherlands

    b. Why the Netherlands became famous for tulips

    c. The importance of tulips to the Dutch economy

    d. An economic bubble in the Netherlands in the early 1600s

Details 2  **According to the passage, which is NOT true?**

    a. Tulips are not native to the Netherlands.

    b. During Tulip Mania, tulips were overpriced in value.

    c. Only wealthy people got involved in Tulip Mania.

    d. Tulip Mania happened according to the law of supply and demand.

3  **In the Netherlands in the 1630s, the prices of tulip bulbs increased due to** _____ .

    a. powerful demand

    b. their extreme rarity

    c. competitive suppliers

    d. the government's economic policies

4  **During Tulip Mania, why did people in the Netherlands buy tulip bulbs?**

    a. To plant the bulbs

    b. To make profits

    c. To create rare versions

    d. To send them to other countries

Write the answers in complete sentences.

5  **According to the law of supply and demand, when do prices stabilize?**

_____

6  **During Tulip Mania, why did some people begin to sell their tulips?**

_____

# SHOW YOUR COMPREHENSION

**Fill in the chart with the phrases from the box.**

Tulip Mania

| What It Is | • a period in the Netherlands when the prices of tulip bulbs ❶_____ |
|---|---|
| Causes | • Tulips became ❷_____ and were traded at high prices.<br>• ❸_____ raised the prices of tulip bulbs.<br>• People began to buy tulips to ❹_____ . |
| Results | • As the demand for tulips did not last, prices dropped, and many tulips ❺_____ . |

a symbol of high status     the increase in demand

make large profits     rose and dropped rapidly     became worthless

# SUMMARIZE YOUR READING

**Complete the summary with the words from the box.**

increased     last long     prices     high prices

overpriced     got involved     poor     trading products

Tulip Mania was a period in which the ❶_____ of tulip bulbs increased and dropped rapidly. In the Netherlands in the 1630s, rare types of tulips were valued and traded at ❷_____ . Soon, the demand for tulips ❸_____ , which raised their prices even more. Tulips became popular ❹_____ among traders and speculators. Seeing them as an easy way to make profits, more people ❺_____ . However, some people started to realize that tulips were ❻_____ . They doubted that the demand for tulips would ❼_____ . Eventually, prices began to drop, leaving many people ❽_____ .

# Treasures in a Cave

**WARM UP**
1. What type of art did prehistoric people make?
2. How old do you think cave paintings are?

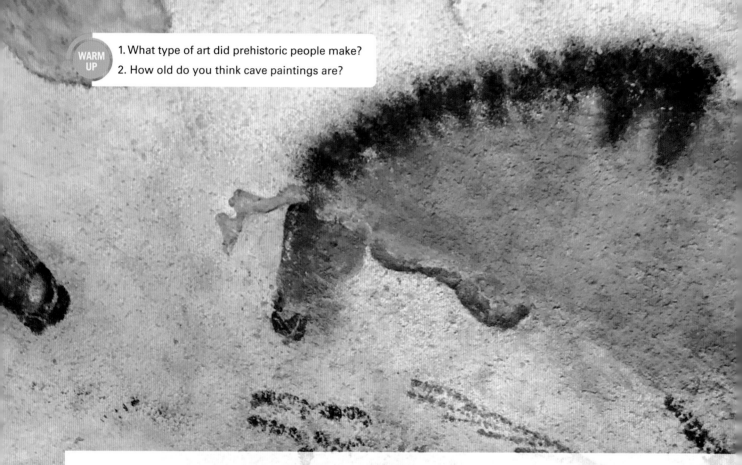

## BEFORE YOU READ

**A  Match the words with the definitions below.**

1. _____ motivate
2. _____ figure
3. _____ ritual
4. _____ sensation
5. _____ replica
6. _____ prehistoric

a. done as a part of a ceremony
b. an exact copy of something
c. the shape of a person's body
d. to make someone want to do something
e. an event that causes great interest or excitement
f. relating to the time before history was written down

**B  Background Knowledge**

Cave paintings can be found all over the world. There are about 400 sites and much of the art was done tens of thousands of years ago. Cave painters mostly used red and black pigments. They painted various animals, figures, and handprints. The cave environment helped to preserve this art for centuries.

Long ago, there was a legend about a secret tunnel leading to a lost treasure. This legend **motivated** 18-year-old Marcel Ravidat to go on an adventure. One day, in 1940, he was out exploring with his dog when he found a deep hole. He thought he had found the

5 entrance to the tunnel and returned with three friends. Together, they entered and found a cave full of wall paintings. They had discovered the Lascaux Cave.

The Lascaux Cave complex is located in southwest France. The paintings were the creations of *Paleolithic people. They are

10 estimated to be more than 17,000 years old. The images mainly show animals, some abstract designs, and a few human-looking **figures**. The actual purpose of the paintings is not known. Some researchers think that they could have been used to pass on information. Others believe that these images had **ritual** purposes.

15 After being discovered, Lascaux became a **sensation** and was opened to the public in 1948. Back then, no one considered preserving the cave. As a result, a large number of visitors caused a huge amount of damage to the paintings. Finally, in 1963, Lascaux was closed to the public in order to preserve the art. Then, in 1983,

20 Lascaux II was opened to the public.

Lascaux II is a **replica** of the cave complex. It was constructed to resemble the two most

25 famous sections and is located near the real Lascaux Cave. Today, only a few scientific experts

▲ Wall paintings in Lascaux Cave

are allowed to enter the real caves. Although most people are not

30 able to see the original paintings, the reproductions look like the originals. If you are interested in **prehistoric** art, Lascaux II can show you what it was like.   Words 283

*****Paleolithic** relating to the time when humans used stone tools and weapons

Q
**What is the paragraph mainly about?**

P1 How
_____
discovered the Lascaux Cave

P2 The wall
_____ inside the Lascaux Cave

P3 How the cave paintings got (moved / damaged)

P4 An important
_____ of the cave complex

# CHECK YOUR COMPREHENSION

Choose the best answers.

<u>Main idea</u>  **1**  **What is the passage mainly about?**

   a. Some famous prehistoric cave paintings

   b. The importance of the Lascaux Cave paintings

   c. The adventures of Marcel Ravidat and his friends

   d. The discovery of the Lascaux Cave and its paintings

<u>Details</u>  **2**  **The Lascaux Cave was found by Marcel Ravidat while he was looking for**

   _____.

   a. a secret tunnel

   b. his dog

   c. Lascaux II

   d. prehistoric cave paintings

**3**  **According to the passage, which is NOT true?**

   a. The Lascaux Cave paintings were discovered in 1940.

   b. The purpose of the Lascaux Cave paintings is unclear.

   c. The Lascaux Cave was open to the public from 1948 to 1963.

   d. Today, no one is allowed to enter the Lascaux Cave.

**4**  **What CANNOT be inferred about Lascaux II?**

   a. It is located in France.

   b. The paintings in Lascaux II are not real.

   c. Tourists have been able to visit it since 1983.

   d. People can see all of the Lascaux Cave paintings there.

Write the answers in complete sentences.

**5**  **What do the paintings in the Lascaux Cave show?**

   _____

**6**  **Why was the Lascaux Cave complex closed to the public?**

   _____

# SHOW YOUR COMPREHENSION

**Fill in the chart with the phrases from the box.**

Lascaux Cave

| Discovery | • found by four teenagers in 1940 in France |
|---|---|
| The Cave Paintings | • painted by ①_____<br>• show ②_____, and human-looking figures<br>• possibly used for rituals or ③_____ |
| Lascaux II | • ④_____ led to the closing of the Lascaux Cave.<br>• In 1983, Lascaux II, a replica of Lascaux, was ⑤_____. |

animals, abstract designs      the damage caused by visitors

opened to the public      Paleolithic people      passing on information

# SUMMARIZE YOUR READING

**Complete the summary with the words from the box.**

purpose      resemble      tunnel      damage

animals      were discovered      open      figures

The Lascaux Cave and its paintings ①_____ by four French teenagers in 1940. They found the paintings while they were looking for a secret ②_____ leading to a lost treasure. The paintings are of ③_____, abstract designs, and human-looking ④_____. The actual ⑤_____ of the paintings is not clear. The cave was once ⑥_____ to the public, but it was closed after the visitors caused a lot of ⑦_____ to the paintings. However, in 1983, Lascaux II was constructed to ⑧_____ part of the original cave. It is open for the public to see.

**Q** **What Treasures Help Us Understand the Past Better?**

STEP 1    **DISCUSSION**    **Talk to your partner and answer the questions.**

1.  What do you think the greatest treasure in your country is?

2. Why do you think it is the greatest?

STEP 2    **ORGANIZATION**    **Fill in the chart with the phrases from the box.**

| | |
|---|---|
| protect Qin Shi Huang | understanding the Egyptian language |
| writing on it in two languages | understand the religions of that time |
| in some caves near the Dead Sea | information about the Chinese emperor |

| | |
|---|---|
| **Introduction** | There are several treasures that help us understand the past better. |
| **Body** | **Supporting sentence 1:** The Rosetta Stone is a stone with _____, ancient Egyptian and Greek. |
| | **Details:** It became the key to _____. |
| | **Supporting sentence 2:** The Terracotta Warriors are statues that were made to _____ in the afterlife. |
| | **Details:** They have given us more _____. |
| | **Supporting sentence 3:** The Dead Sea Scrolls are ancient religious writings found _____. |
| | **Details:** They have helped us _____. |
| **Conclusion** | The Rosetta Stone, the Terracotta Warriors, and the Dead Sea Scrolls have given us a better understanding of human history. |

**FIRST DRAFT** **Complete the writing with the phrases from the chart.**

Title What Treasures Help Us Understand the Past Better?

There are several treasures that help us understand the past better.

First of all, the Rosetta Stone is a stone with _____ , ancient Egyptian and Greek. It became the key to _____ .

Second, the Terracotta Warriors are statues that were made to _____ in the afterlife. They have given us more _____ .

Lastly, the Dead Sea Scrolls are ancient religious writings found _____ . They have helped us _____ .

In conclusion, the Rosetta Stone, the Terracotta Warriors, and the Dead Sea Scrolls have given us a better understanding of human history.

**FINAL DRAFT** **Complete the writing. Replace one of the details with your own idea.**

Title _____

There are several treasures that help us understand the past better.

First of all, _____
_____

Second, _____
_____

Lastly, _____
_____

In conclusion, _____
_____

**MEMO**

MEMO

# Reading for Subject

SECOND EDITION

## Workbook

### 3

DARAKWON

School Subject-Integrated Reading Series

# Reading for Subject

SECOND EDITION

**Workbook**

**3**

# ┃ VOCABULARY PRACTICE

A   **Write the correct words for the definitions.**

| | | | | |
|---|---|---|---|---|
| ash | debris | molten | inactive | note |

1.  broken pieces of something larger                              _____

2.  not able to erupt or explode                                    _____

3.  to mention; to give attention to                               _____

4.  being in a liquid state because of high heat                   _____

5.  gray or black powder that is left after something burns        _____

B   **Choose the word that has a meaning similar to the underlined word.**

1.  The strong winds created sand <u>dunes</u> on the beach.

    a. hills            b. pits            c. mountains            d. ponds

2.  Children <u>encounter</u> many challenges when they start school.

    a. speak            b. face            c. fight            d. damage

C   **Complete the sentences with the words in the box.**

| | | | | |
|---|---|---|---|---|
| associated | slopes | plywood | enthusiast | thrill seekers |

1.  They ski down the snowy _____ near the resort.

2.  Many _____ enjoy bungee jumping and sky diving.

3.  They built the tree house from pieces of old _____.

4.  He considers himself to be an ancient history _____.

5.  There are many side effects _____ with taking that medicine.

# ⌶ SENTENCE PRACTICE

**D** **Translate the sentences into your language, focusing on the meanings of the underlined parts.**

1. Some riders prefer to stand <u>while</u> others like to sit.

   _____

2. There are a few dangers <u>associated with</u> volcano surfing.

   _____

3. Still, the sport remains dangerous <u>with</u> only the bravest <u>attempting</u> it.

   _____

4. The second type of volcano surfing is less dangerous <u>since</u> riders use the slopes of inactive volcanoes.

   _____

**E** **Unscramble the words to complete the sentences.**

1. goggles / shield / ash and debris / can / their eyes / from

   _____

2. popular / volcano surfing / the years / among / became / over / thrill seekers

   _____

3. should / stay safe, / wear / volcano surfers / protective gear / special

   To _____

4. takes / danger / volcano surfing / that idea / in terms of / to the next level

   _____

# I VOCABULARY PRACTICE

### A   Write the correct words for the definitions.

| adaptation | nectar | scent | defend | rotten |
|---|---|---|---|---|

1. to fight off; to protect      _____

2. the smell something makes      _____

3. a sugary liquid made by flowers      _____

4. the state of being broken down; decayed      _____

5. a change that helps a living thing survive      _____

### B   Choose the word that has a meaning similar to the underlined word.

1. You resemble your father very closely.

   a. misunderstand      b. grow up      c. follow      d. look like

2. Rotten eggs usually give off a very bad smell.

   a. release      b. take in      c. express      d. absorb

### C   Complete the sentences with the words in the box.

| organisms | surroundings | attract | imitating | responded |
|---|---|---|---|---|

1. He _____ by sending an email to his cousin.

2. This university wants to _____ hardworking students.

3. You can improve your English by _____ native speakers.

4. Chameleons can change colors according to their _____.

5. The _____ are so small that they can only be seen under a microscope.

# ┊ SENTENCE PRACTICE

D   **Translate the sentences into your language, focusing on the meanings of the underlined parts.**

1. Other plants survive <u>by imitating</u> their surroundings.

   _____

2. Through this, the plant <u>prevents</u> butterflies <u>from</u> laying eggs on its leaves.

   _____

3. Scents <u>made by</u> plants can also be used to defend against or to attract insects.

   _____

4. Additionally, plants have developed various systems <u>to increase</u> their chances of survival.

   _____

E   **Unscramble the words to complete the sentences.**

1. them / this / predators / safe / keeps / from

   _____

2. pollinators / flies and beetles / this odor / like / attracts

   _____

3. nearby flowers / helps them / nectar / that have / resemble

   Mimicry _____

4. plants / of things / use mimicry / around them / the traits / to copy

   _____

# ⏐ VOCABULARY PRACTICE

A   **Write the correct words for the definitions.**

| priest | poverty | servant | urban | rank |
| --- | --- | --- | --- | --- |

1.  relating to a town or city                          _____

2.  the state of being poor                          _____

3.  one's position in a society or group          _____

4.  a person who serves others                     _____

5.  someone who performs religious duties     _____

B   **Choose the word that has a meaning similar to the underlined word.**

1.  The children should be <u>divided</u> into four teams to play the game.

    a. added              b. separated          c. moved              d. exchanged

2.  The teacher <u>viewed</u> his students as leaders of the future.

    a. saw                b. praised            c. asked              d. informed

C   **Complete the sentences with the words in the box.**

| belong to | exist | original | community | discriminated |
| --- | --- | --- | --- | --- |

1.  The _____ price of this product was very high.

2.  The artist is a member of the local creative _____.

3.  Jina does not _____ our group, but she wants to join it.

4.  The worker argued that his employer _____ against him.

5.  The dinosaurs are extinct, so they do not _____ anymore.

# ❙ SENTENCE PRACTICE

D   **Translate the sentences into your language, focusing on the meanings of the underlined parts.**

1.  Different forms of the caste system <u>have been found</u> in various cultures.

    _____

2.  People do <u>not</u> choose <u>what</u> caste they belong to <u>but</u> are born into one.

    _____

3.  Many times, <u>the way</u> people are viewed and treated by others depends on their castes.

    _____

4.  In modern India, there are laws <u>to protect</u> the Untouchables, but many are still discriminated against.

    _____

E   **Unscramble the words to complete the sentences.**

1.  Indian society / into / divided / called *jatis* / is / numerous communities

    _____

2.  divides people / a caste system / is / that / a social structure / into groups

    _____

3.  the merchants / who / the Vaishyas / were / owned / and farmers / their own farms

    _____

4.  in modern India / than in urban ones / is / prominent / in rural areas / more

    The caste system _____

# ┃ VOCABULARY PRACTICE

A **Write the correct words for the definitions.**

| contemporary | display | rot | preserve | unstable |

1. to show; to exhibit _____
2. to decay gradually _____
3. not strong, firm, or safe _____
4. to save; to keep in good condition _____
5. relating to things happening now or recently _____

B **Choose the word that has a meaning similar to the underlined word.**

1. They held a <u>competition</u> to see who the best singer was.

   a. party          b. event          c. test          d. contest

2. This old house always feels so cold, dark, and <u>depressing</u>.

   a. creepy          b. impressive          c. sad          d. lively

C **Complete the sentences with the words in the box.**

| seats | serves | resources | structure | originally |

1. Archaeologists found a strange _____ in the jungle.

2. Water is one of the most important natural _____.

3. He was _____ cast as the villain in this musical.

4. This building _____ as a shelter when there is a disaster.

5. The wedding hall comfortably _____ at least 150 people.

# ❙ SENTENCE PRACTICE

D **Translate the sentences into your language, focusing on the meanings of the underlined parts.**

1. An abandoned building can <u>make an area seem</u> depressing and lonely.

2. Today, it remains <u>one of the world's most popular</u> modern art galleries.

3. <u>Built</u> in Cape Town in 1921, the building was first a grain silo complex until 2001.

4. It was reopened <u>as</u> a bookstore <u>called</u> El Ateneo Grand Splendid in 2000.

E **Unscramble the words to complete the sentences.**

1. repurposed / the building's history / some / to preserve / are

2. it / in 1891 / a power plant / built / was / originally

3. in the first year alone / with millions of people / reopened / visiting it / in 2000

    The building _____

4. the theater / and held / over a thousand people / a variety of / could seat / performances

# VOCABULARY PRACTICE

A **Write the correct words for the definitions.**

| guide | solid | capture | vehicle | flight |
|---|---|---|---|---|

1. to catch                                          _____

2. hard; not liquid                                  _____

3. an aircraft's journey                             _____

4. to lead; to direct                               _____

5. a machine that transports people and things       _____

B **Choose the word that has a meaning similar to the underlined word.**

1. It is <u>commonly</u> cloudy and rainy in London, England.

   a. unfortunately      b. usually          c. slightly          d. wildly

2. They <u>collected</u> seashells when they visited the beach last summer.

   a. cleaned           b. found            c. traded            d. gathered

C **Complete the sentences with the words in the box.**

| features | explored | programmed | riverbed | equipment |
|---|---|---|---|---|

1. The robots are _____ to cook and clean the house.

2. It is safest for crayfish to live close to the _____.

3. You need a lot of _____ to go camping for three weeks.

4. The children _____ the abandoned factory all afternoon.

5. This new smartphone has many interesting _____ and apps.

# ▌SENTENCE PRACTICE

D  **Translate the sentences into your language, focusing on the meanings of the underlined parts.**

1. These important features could <u>help</u> scientists <u>understand how</u> life began on Earth.

   _____

2. The temperature is <u>so low that</u> a person would freeze to death in seconds.

   _____

3. Dragonfly is programmed to guide itself <u>since</u> NASA <u>will not be flying</u> it remotely.

   _____

4. Titan, its largest, has captured the attention of <u>many who</u> are interested in space exploration.

   _____

E  **Unscramble the words to complete the sentences.**

1. for the drone / NASA / to make / intends / short flights

   _____

2. far less / the cost / than sending / is / a human team / of sending a drone

   Additionally, _____

3. why is / important step / such an / in space exploration / Dragonfly

   _____

4. about Titan's surface / scientists on Earth / and composition / all they can / will learn

   _____

# VOCABULARY PRACTICE

A  **Write the correct words for the definitions.**

| cure | variety | pass on | tribe | custom |
|------|---------|---------|-------|--------|

1.  to stop a disease _____

2.  to teach a younger generation something _____

3.  a number of different things of the same type _____

4.  a traditional way of doing something _____

5.  a traditional society that shares a culture or ancestors _____

B  **Choose the word that has a meaning similar to the underlined word.**

1.  Eating a balanced diet is <u>essential</u> to staying healthy.

    a. useful          b. harmful          c. vital          d. uncertain

2.  Mother birds <u>frequently</u> leave the nest to gather food for their babies.

    a. always          b. quickly          c. rarely          d. often

C  **Complete the sentences with the words in the box.**

| depend upon | involves | aspect | syllables | upcoming |
|-------------|----------|--------|-----------|----------|

1.  "Rabbit" is a word that has two _____ .

2.  Food is an important _____ of every culture.

3.  Whether we play baseball or not will _____ the weather.

4.  He turned down the job offer because it _____ a lot of travel.

5.  The manager is in charge of posting _____ events on our website.

# I SENTENCE PRACTICE

D   **Translate the sentences into your language, focusing on the meanings of the underlined parts.**

1. Men and women also have different roles <u>when it comes to</u> music.

 

2. Simply put, music <u>is of great importance to</u> Native American life.

 

3. On the other hand, women sing songs to their children <u>that</u> are about lighter topics.

 

4. Most Native Americans <u>consider</u> singing <u>to be</u> the most essential aspect of Native American music.

 

E   **Unscramble the words to complete the sentences.**

1. a wide variety of / also use / to make music / instruments

   Most _____

2. the sounds / which tribe / depend upon / they produce / made them

 

3. have songs / diseases / they even / can cure / that they believe

 

4. to new generations / their customs / pass on / through their songs / and history

   They _____

# ┃ VOCABULARY PRACTICE

**A**   **Write the correct words for the definitions.**

| theorist | sociable | self-centered | pay attention to | sibling |
|----------|----------|---------------|------------------|---------|

1.  one's sister or brother                                          _____

2.  focused on or caring only about oneself                          _____

3.  good in social situations; outgoing                              _____

4.  a person who develops ideas and makes theories                   _____

5.  to watch or listen to something or someone carefully             _____


**B**   **Choose the word that has a meaning similar to the underlined word.**

1.  No one can <u>predict</u> how the presidential election will turn out.

    a. explain          b. foresee          c. change          d. limit

2.  Darwin's <u>theory</u> of evolution is widely accepted by scientists.

    a. concept          b. story            c. experiment      d. gift


**C**   **Complete the sentences with the words in the box.**

| please | left out | entertained | charming | responsible |
|--------|----------|-------------|----------|-------------|

1.  A powerful leader is _____ and charismatic.

2.  The actor is shown as a(n) _____ man in the movie.

3.  The magician _____ the children with many tricks.

4.  He thought of buying some flowers to _____ his girlfriend.

5.  Carol felt _____ when she was not invited to the birthday party.

# ❙ SENTENCE PRACTICE

D   **Translate the sentences into your language, focusing on the meanings of the underlined parts.**

1. He was one of the first theorists <u>to suggest</u> the birth order theory.

   _____

2. <u>Not everyone</u> believes the birth order theory is perfect though.

   _____

3. <u>So can</u> conditions such as the family's income and <u>how</u> parents raise their children.

   _____

4. Lastly, only children have personalities similar to <u>those</u> of <u>either</u> oldest <u>or</u> youngest children.

   _____

   _____

E   **Unscramble the words to complete the sentences.**

1. who / was / did research / in the early 1900s / a psychologist / Alfred Adler

   _____

2. he believed / of children / develop / affects / the birth order / how their personalities

   _____

3. they / to get / charming or funny / attention / from their parents / try / by being

   _____

4. according to / a child's personality / cannot always / was born / predict / when he or she

   People _____

# | VOCABULARY PRACTICE

**A** **Write the correct words for the definitions.**

| honor | free | announce | come to an end | movement |

1. to make something known publicly _____

2. to conclude or finish something _____

3. to release from prison, slavery, or suffering _____

4. to show respect toward a person or an achievement _____

5. a group of people acting as one to achieve a common goal _____

**B** **Choose the word that has a meaning similar to the underlined word.**

1. The pilot had a long <u>military</u> career.

   a. organization     b. community     c. station     d. army

2. The city will hold an <u>election</u> in February to choose a new mayor.

   a. vote     b. event     c. feast     d. meeting

**C** **Complete the sentences with the words in the box.**

| jail | equally | release | get involved in | nonviolent |

1. She doesn't want to _____ political activities.

2. The man spent seven years in _____ for robbing a bank.

3. Camille wants her and her brother to be treated _____.

4. There are many _____ ways to protest something.

5. The rescue group will _____ the foxes into the wild.

# ! SENTENCE PRACTICE

D   **Translate the sentences into your language, focusing on the meanings of the underlined parts.**

1.  <u>It</u> was his school teacher <u>who</u> later gave him the English name Nelson.

   _____

2.  This <u>led</u> Mandela <u>to</u> start a military group <u>to fight</u> against the government.

   _____

3.  He was sent to jail several times <u>until</u> he was finally sentenced to life imprisonment.

   _____

4.  Mandela was respected and honored <u>not only</u> by the people of South Africa <u>but</u> by people all over the world.

   _____

E   **Unscramble the words to complete the sentences.**

1.  Black South Africans / he / to free / without / wanted / using violence

   _____

2.  began / with the president / to negotiate / he also / to end Apartheid

   _____

3.  Mandela / the Nobel Peace Prize / his work / was awarded / for

   In 1993, _____

4.  Mandela / to other countries / and continued / nonviolent resistance / believed in / to spread his ideas

   _____

# ǀ VOCABULARY PRACTICE

### A    Write the correct words for the definitions.

| reserve | live off | poison | appearance | hunting ground |
|---------|----------|--------|------------|----------------|

1. how something looks                                    _____

2. an area of land that is protected                      _____

3. the area in which an animal hunts for food             _____

4. to survive by eating a particular type of food         _____

5. a substance that can kill or injure a living thing     _____

### B    Choose the word that has a meaning similar to the underlined word.

1. Cars now use GPS to help people <u>locate</u> their destinations.

   a. share              b. save              c. change              d. find

2. There are many species of frog living in this <u>creek</u>.

   a. lake               b. well              c. stream              d. fountain

### C    Complete the sentences with the words in the box.

| young | native to | species | prior to | mammals |
|-------|-----------|---------|----------|---------|

1. Coral reefs are home to millions of different _____.

2. Many people do not realize that whales are _____.

3. _____ graduating, you have to pass your exams.

4. Lions are large cats that are _____ Africa and India.

5. Mother birds feed their _____ worms and insects.

# ┃ SENTENCE PRACTICE

D    **Translate the sentences into your language, focusing on the meanings of the underlined parts.**

1. <u>Upon seeing</u> one, most people are shocked by the animal's strange appearance.

   _____

2. Each platypus has a duck-like bill<u>, which</u> is soft and wet and <u>helps</u> the animal <u>find</u> food.

   _____

3. Since they <u>keep</u> their eyes and ears <u>closed</u> in the water, they use their bills to feel and locate prey there.

   _____

4. Droughts and forest fires are destroying their homes, <u>leaving</u> them without protection or food.

   _____


E    **Unscramble the words to complete the sentences.**

1. killed / on land / are often / by dingoes / that look for food

   Platypus _____

2. help them / front feet / through the water / their webbed / move efficiently

   _____

3. between 1-1.5 kg / are / most platypus / in length / and weigh / only about 40-50 cm

   _____

4. their stingers during mating season / they use / who enter / to fight / their territory / other males

   _____

# VOCABULARY PRACTICE

A  **Write the correct words for the definitions.**

| concern | fair | win | by surprise | last |
|---------|------|-----|-------------|------|

1. unexpectedly  _____

2. very beautiful or attractive  _____

3. to relate to something  _____

4. to continue for a period of time  _____

5. to achieve victory in a war, game, etc.  _____

B  **Choose the word that has a meaning similar to the underlined word.**

1. Mothers tell their children many kinds of <u>legends</u>.

   a. movies          b. tales          c. promises          d. excuses

2. My classmate Mike <u>comes up with</u> good ideas all the time.

   a. goes to          b. looks after          c. thinks up          d. picks up

C  **Complete the sentences with the words in the box.**

| rest | goddess | votes | stormed | pretended |
|------|---------|-------|---------|-----------|

1. Aphrodite is known as the _____ of love and beauty.

2. Politicians make many promises to win our _____.

3. He _____ from the classroom after failing the final exam.

4. Tom didn't know the answer to the question but _____ to.

5. The _____ of his life was unhappy after his business failed.

# I SENTENCE PRACTICE

D   **Translate the sentences into your language, focusing on the meanings of the underlined parts.**

1. <u>Even though</u> Helen was already married to Menelaus, that did not stop Aphrodite.

_____

2. Paris accepted Aphrodite's offering <u>of</u> the most beautiful woman in the world, Helen.

_____

3. Some Greek warriors hid inside a giant wooden horse they <u>had built</u> <u>while</u> the rest of the army pretended to leave.

_____

4. <u>Offended,</u> Eris stormed into the wedding and threw a golden apple with the words "For the Fairest" <u>inscribed</u> on it.

_____

E   **Unscramble the words to complete the sentences.**

1. for help / that Helen was gone, / he asked / Menelaus learned / his brother

   Once _____

2. assembled / to Troy / Agamemnon / and set off / a rescue force

   _____

3. until Odysseus / lasted / came up with / for ten years / the Trojan Horse / the idea for

   The war _____

4. concerns / the legend / between the Greeks / a mythological war / of the Trojan War / and the city of Troy

   _____

# I VOCABULARY PRACTICE

A   **Write the correct words for the definitions.**

| battered | prison | criminal | threat | form |
|---|---|---|---|---|

1. to make or create something      _____

2. a person who commits a crime      _____

3. having been harmed by another person repeatedly      _____

4. the possibility that something very bad will happen      _____

5. a place that holds people who are being punished for a crime      _____

B   **Choose the word that has a meaning similar to the underlined word.**

1. The vet formed a <u>bond</u> with the rescued animals.

   a. test       b. relationship       c. event       d. contract

2. She felt that her parents did not see the <u>positive</u> side of the situation.

   a. good       b. poor       c. exciting       d. harmful

C   **Complete the sentences with the words in the box.**

| emotional | victims | cooperate | kindness | survive |
|---|---|---|---|---|

1. We need to _____ to find the best solution.

2. Plants cannot _____ without water and sunlight.

3. They provided the flood _____ with food and clothing.

4. Doctors say physical health is connected to _____ health.

5. The employees treat their customers with respect and _____.

# SENTENCE PRACTICE

D Translate the sentences into your language, focusing on the meanings of the underlined parts.

1. Then, they start behaving in ways to please their captor.

2. They even started to think of the police as their enemy.

3. Swedish doctor Nils Bejerot gave their condition the name Stockholm Syndrome.

4. Four people were taken hostage in a bank by Jan-Erik Olsson, who had just gotten out of prison.

E Unscramble the words to complete the sentences.

1. does not / Stockholm Syndrome / happen / in a hostage situation / to everyone

2. did not / with the efforts / cooperate / to rescue them / the hostages

   Surprisingly, _____

3. threatened / some kindness / to kill / but also / showed them / the hostages

   The two criminals _____

4. from an incident / in 1973 / Stockholm Syndrome / that happened / got its name / in Stockholm, Sweden,

# ❙ VOCABULARY PRACTICE

A **Write the correct words for the definitions.**

| emphasize | drip | unconscious | artwork | influential |
|---|---|---|---|---|

1. a piece of art created by an artist      _____

2. having a great effect on something      _____

3. to drop liquid onto something      _____

4. to give special importance to something      _____

5. the mind's hidden thoughts and feelings      _____

B **Choose the word that has a meaning similar to the underlined word.**

1. Facial expressions are used to <u>convey</u> one's emotions.

   a. imagine      b. affect      c. entertain      d. communicate

2. Many herbs are used to <u>heal</u> illnesses in Eastern medicine.

   a. mix      b. change      c. cure      d. transform

C **Complete the sentences with the words in the box.**

| physical | energetically | focuses on | splashing | related |
|---|---|---|---|---|

1. Look at the children _____ around in the pool.

2. He _____ answered the interviewer's questions.

3. Most of my stress is _____ to the assignment.

4. The test _____ grammar rather than conversation skills.

5. Abstract art looks much different from the _____ world.

# ❙ SENTENCE PRACTICE

**D** **Translate the sentences into your language, focusing on the meanings of the underlined parts.**

1. Instead, he just <u>let</u> his thoughts and emotions <u>lead</u> him.

   _____

2. These lines <u>show</u> viewers <u>how</u> he moved his body while painting.

   _____

3. This <u>allows</u> the viewers <u>to</u> have their own understanding and interpretations of the artwork.

   _____

4. Action painters helped people express <u>what</u> they wanted to say when they could not find the right words.

   _____

**E** **Unscramble the words to complete the sentences.**

1. how / to look / did not plan / his paintings / he wanted

   He _____

2. the physical action / an important part / is itself / of painting / of the finished work

   _____

3. get rid of / a new kind of art / they needed / to help them / their pain / heal and

   _____

4. famous / curving lines and shapes / which created / for his dripping method, / across the canvas

   He was _____

# ❚ VOCABULARY PRACTICE

A  **Write the correct words for the definitions.**

| earn | poisonous | novelist | philosopher | request |

1. the act of asking for something      _____

2. a person who writes novels      _____

3. to get something by doing work      _____

4. someone who studies the meaning of life      _____

5. causing illness or death, often coming from a plant or chemical      _____

B  **Choose the word that has a meaning similar to the underlined word.**

1. The movie received praise from several <u>critics</u>.

   a. authors          b. reviewers          c. publishers          d. lawyers

2. Some parents choose to <u>educate</u> their children at home.

   a. teach          b. award          c. scold          d. assess

C  **Complete the sentences with the words in the box.**

| publish | unable | realistically | suffer from | broke out |

1. The film _____ shows life after the war.

2. A fight _____ between two groups of students.

3. The school will _____ a book of the students' poetry.

4. Some people _____ spring allergies and may sneeze a lot.

5. Color blind people are _____ to distinguish between certain colors.

# ❘ SENTENCE PRACTICE

D   **Translate the sentences into your language, focusing on the meanings of the underlined parts.**

1.   It was <u>so</u> successful <u>that</u> a second volume was published.

   _____

2.   She wrote about her personal experiences with her three sisters <u>while growing up</u>.

   _____

3.   She later edited these letters and published them in a book <u>titled</u> *Hospital Sketches*.

   _____

4.   She took any job <u>available</u>, but she often <u>worked as</u> a domestic servant or a teacher.

   _____

E   **Unscramble the words to complete the sentences.**

1.   writing / she / stories / enjoyed / and plays / as a child,

   _____

2.   was / an educator and philosopher, / a decent living / to make / unable

   Louisa's father, _____

3.   she was / by her father / family friends / and also learned / educated / from
   prominent

   _____

4.   she also / and short stories / to earn / started writing poems / for magazines / some
   money

   _____

# ⏐ VOCABULARY PRACTICE

**A** **Write the correct words for the definitions.**

| arrow | crop | drag | flower | messenger |
|---|---|---|---|---|

1. to force someone to go somewhere      _____

2. a person who delivers messages      _____

3. to produce new buds, often in spring      _____

4. the fruits, vegetables, and grains grown on a farm      _____

5. a long weapon with a pointed tip that is shot from a bow      _____

**B** **Choose the word that has a meaning similar to the underlined word.**

1. The Sahara Desert is so <u>infertile</u> that farmers cannot grow crops there.

   a. wild      b. barren      c. moist      d. vast

2. More than 300 families were <u>reunited</u> after being separated for a year.

   a. brought together      b. excluded from      c. relocated to      d. torn apart

**C** **Complete the sentences with the words in the box.**

| harvest | realized | mention | livestock | underworld |
|---|---|---|---|---|

1. Now that you _____ it, I remember meeting her.

2. Some believe the soul goes to the _____ after someone dies.

3. I _____ after I failed the test that I should have studied harder.

4. He raises _____ such as chickens, pigs, and cows for a living.

5. Thanks to the good weather, farmers can enjoy a good _____ this year.

# | SENTENCE PRACTICE

D  **Translate the sentences into your language, focusing on the meanings of the underlined parts.**

1.  Hades <u>had no choice but to</u> obey Zeus.

   _____

2.  He <u>had been hit by</u> one of Eros's arrows and lost his heart to Persephone.

   _____

3.  Before sending Persephone away, Hades <u>tricked</u> her <u>into</u> eating some pomegranate seeds.

   _____

4.  Demeter loved her daughter <u>so much that</u> when she was gone, the land became cold and infertile.

   _____

E  **Unscramble the words to complete the sentences.**

1.  flowered again / Persephone returned, / to welcome / plants / her / when

   _____

2.  there are / the story of Persephone / why / explains / different seasons

   _____

3.  the underworld / with her mother / four months in / and the rest of the year / would spend

   Persephone _____

4.  if someone / had to / while in the underworld, / he or she / ate something / stay forever

   He knew that _____

# I VOCABULARY PRACTICE

A   **Write the correct words for the definitions.**

| fame | rework | complete | unsolved | sore |
|------|--------|----------|----------|------|

1. the state of being famous _____

2. being in pain; aching _____

3. to finish something _____

4. remaining a mystery _____

5. to change or alter something, usually a piece of art _____

B   **Choose the word that has a meaning similar to the underlined word.**

1. She had a <u>rough</u> time after her father's death.

   a. smooth          b. uncertain          c. rich          d. difficult

2. The children needed <u>constant</u> attention from the babysitter.

   a. unsteady          b. extreme          c. continuous          d. serious

C   **Complete the sentences with the words in the box.**

| competition | based on | experimental | heroine | unfortunately |
|-------------|----------|--------------|---------|---------------|

1. _____, the shoes I wanted to buy were sold out.

2. Her novel was _____ her experience of the war.

3. The actress is qualified enough to be the _____ of the movie.

4. My sister is planning to take part in the national dance _____.

5. The technology for human cloning is still in the _____ stage.

# I SENTENCE PRACTICE

D   **Translate the sentences into your language, focusing on the meanings of the underlined parts.**

1.  During surgery, there were some complications, which <u>led to him having</u> a heart attack.

2.  His next work was *Tosca<u>, which</u>* is known for its well-organized plot and beautiful lyrics.

3.  <u>It was not until</u> he saw a performance of Verdi's *Aida* <u>that</u> he decided to become an opera composer.

4.  <u>It was said that</u> he was always in love with a new woman <u>whenever</u> he wrote a new opera.

E   **Unscramble the words to complete the sentences.**

1.  was / an unsolved mystery / who / remains / the actual person

2.  him / Puccini's success / but also / gave / a lot of money / not only fame

3.  onto his works / images of the women / also said that / he would project / he loved

    It was

4.  constant sore throats / with throat cancer / he began / and was later / suffering from / diagnosed

    However,

# ┃ VOCABULARY PRACTICE

A    **Write the correct words for the definitions.**

| physics    humanity    award    attendee    state |

1. to say; to declare                          _____

2. to give a prize                             _____

3. the study of matter and energy              _____

4. a person who goes to an event               _____

5. the condition of being a human              _____

B    **Choose the word that has a meaning similar to the underlined word.**

1. Pizza is a <u>well-known</u> food that originally came from Italy.

   a. famous          b. distinct          c. delicious          d. inventive

2. Graduating from university is a great <u>achievement</u>.

   a. disappointment    b. environment      c. accomplishment    d. contentment

C    **Complete the sentences with the words in the box.**

| tradition    magnetism    ceremony    trivial    humorous |

1. Decorating a tree is a common Christmas _____.

2. The awards _____ will be held in the theater.

3. Some theories try to explain what causes Earth's _____.

4. The play was so _____ that everyone kept laughing.

5. The employee thought the customer's complaint was _____.

# ❙ SENTENCE PRACTICE

D  **Translate the sentences into your language, focusing on the meanings of the underlined parts.**

1. On the other hand, <u>what may seem</u> trivial might actually have great benefits.

   _____

2. Rather, it honors research that <u>makes people laugh</u> first and then think.

   _____

3. <u>It</u> is tradition <u>for</u> the attendees <u>to throw</u> paper airplanes onto the stage during the ceremony.

   _____

4. This rule states that food on the floor is still safe <u>to eat</u> <u>if less than</u> five seconds has passed.

   _____

E  **Unscramble the words to complete the sentences.**

1. was / by / the Ig Nobel Prize / a humorous / founded in 1991 / science magazine

   _____

2. recognize research / comical / most Ig Nobel Prizes / that seems / in some way

   _____

3. they have helped / the spread / some African nations / prevent / of malaria

   _____

4. achievements / is / that recognizes / in various subjects / a well-known award

   The Nobel Prize _____

# | VOCABULARY PRACTICE

A **Write the correct words for the definitions.**

| control | eventually | common | worsen | goal |

1. to make something worse _____

2. occurring usually or done often _____

3. an aim or a desired result _____

4. to influence the outcome of something _____

5. happening after some time, in the end _____

B **Choose the word that has a meaning similar to the underlined word.**

1. The <u>rumor</u> about her turned out to be false.

   a. truth          b. photo          c. document          d. gossip

2. She did not eat or drink anything <u>throughout</u> the day.

   a. during          b. before          c. after          d. inside

C **Complete the sentences with the words in the box.**

| lies | celebrities | repeat | unbelievable | imagined |

1. Nobody will trust you if you keep telling _____.

2. He _____ that he would become a movie star.

3. I saw some _____ surrounded by their fans.

4. The best way to memorize words is to _____ them over and over.

5. It is _____ that my mom allowed me to play games all day long.

# ❘ SENTENCE PRACTICE

D **Translate the sentences into your language, focusing on the meanings of the underlined parts.**

1.  Many big lies <u>have been told</u> throughout history and are still told today.

   _____

2.  He was able to <u>convince</u> many non-Jewish Germans <u>that</u> his lies were the truth.

   _____

3.  People come to believe that the big lie is true <u>no matter how</u> shocking it may be.

   _____

4.  The goal of anyone <u>telling</u> a big lie is <u>to influence</u> how people feel or what they think about something.

   _____

E **Unscramble the words to complete the sentences.**

1.  used to spread / a technique / is / the "big lie" / a false idea

   _____

2.  it / common / small lies / is / to tell / for most people

   _____

3.  one of / to be / the minds of others / the best ways / has been proven / to control

   The technique _____

4.  numerous false statements / this discrimination / about them / Hitler worsened / by making

   _____

# I VOCABULARY PRACTICE

A   **Write the correct words for the definitions.**

| nausea | age | excess | intake | brittle |
|---|---|---|---|---|

1. to grow older _____

2. easily broken _____

3. too much of something _____

4. the feeling that you might vomit _____

5. the amount a person eats, drinks, or breathes in _____

B   **Choose the word that has a meaning similar to the underlined word.**

1. Experts say fewer than eight hours of sleep may not be <u>adequate</u>.

   a. impressive      b. incomplete      c. excessive      d. enough

2. There is a <u>connection</u> between climate change and these storms.

   a. link      b. process      c. result      d. effect

C   **Complete the sentences with the words in the box.**

| diabetes | muscle | immune system | ensure | consume |
|---|---|---|---|---|

1. Your _____ helps your body fight off viruses.

2. The hockey player couldn't skate after he pulled a _____.

3. If you want to be stronger, try to _____ more protein.

4. Please _____ you answer the test questions carefully.

5. His blood sugar is unstable because he has _____.

# ▎SENTENCE PRACTICE

D   **Translate the sentences into your language, focusing on the meanings of the underlined parts.**

1. The first is <u>through</u> the skin <u>via</u> exposure to sunlight.

2. A loss of bone might mean brittle bones <u>as</u> a person ages.

3. <u>Having</u> too much vitamin D is usually not caused by food intake or sun exposure.

4. Vitamin D has many benefits <u>that</u> improve bone health <u>as well as</u> your muscles and immune system.

E   **Unscramble the words to complete the sentences.**

1. into your body / three main ways / to get / there are / vitamin D

2. per day / a person needs / depends / the amount / on age / of vitamin D

3. as / health problems / vitamin D / overdo it / can also cause / don't

4. digestive issues / too much vitamin D / lead to / like nausea and vomiting / can

# ⏐ VOCABULARY PRACTICE

**A**   **Write the correct words for the definitions.**

| possession   gain   introduce   luxurious   rare |
|---|

1.  not common _____

2.  something you own _____

3.  to get something _____

4.  very expensive and usually attractive _____

5.  to bring something to an area for the first time _____

**B**   **Choose the word that has a meaning similar to the underlined word.**

1.  She returned to her <u>ordinary</u> life after her long trip.

    a. regular          b. adventurous          c. boring          d. slow

2.  It is the best time to buy a car because the prices have <u>dropped</u>.

    a. risen          b. fallen          c. changed          d. widened

**C**   **Complete the sentences with the words in the box.**

| out of control   amount   determine   varieties   worthless |
|---|

1.  Most old mobile phones are nearly _____.

2.  The car went _____ and hit the tree.

3.  He likes to collect rare _____ of plants.

4.  Put a piece of lemon into a small _____ of water.

5.  My dad spun the egg to _____ if it was hardboiled.

# ❙ SENTENCE PRACTICE

D    **Translate the sentences into your language, focusing on the meanings of the underlined parts.**

1.    Demand is the amount of goods and services <u>that</u> consumers want to buy.

2.    At the time, the demand for tulip bulbs rose <u>so rapidly that</u> prices went out of control.

3.    Eventually, prices dropped, and many <u>were left</u> poor with a supply of tulips <u>that</u> were worthless.

4.    When the amount of goods in demand is <u>the same as</u> the amount of goods <u>being</u> supplied, it stabilizes prices.

E    **Unscramble the words to complete the sentences.**

1.    as / prices / in tulip bulbs, / became interested / more people / rose even more

2.    in order / began selling / some people / to buy them / all of their possessions

3.    the law / goods and services / explains / are determined / how the prices of / of supply and demand

4.    as valuable / at high prices / rare varieties / and were traded / and luxurious items / were seen

       As a result, _____

# ❙ VOCABULARY PRACTICE

### A   Write the correct words for the definitions.

| complex     adventure     construct     reproduction     section |
| --- |

1. to build something              _____

2. a replica or copy of something    _____

3. a fun and exciting journey       _____

4. a portion or area of something larger   _____

5. a group of buildings used for a particular purpose   _____

### B   Choose the word that has a meaning similar to the underlined word.

1. The <u>entrance</u> to the building is closed because of the fire.

   a. basement       b. door       c. terrace       d. barrier

2. The hurricane caused a lot of <u>damage</u> in the area.

   a. pathways       b. benefits       c. debris       d. destruction

### C   Complete the sentences with the words in the box.

| public     creations     estimated     expert     treasures |
| --- |

1. Ask Tom since he is a(n) _____ in computers.

2. The art gallery exhibits the _____ of local artists.

3. The book is _____ to be about 800 years old.

4. A number of _____ were found in the king's tomb.

5. The city library is open to the _____ and welcomes all visitors.

# ❙ SENTENCE PRACTICE

**D**   **Translate the sentences into your language, focusing on the meanings of the underlined parts.**

1.   This legend <u>motivated</u> 18-year-old Marcel Ravidat <u>to</u> go on an adventure.

   _____

2.   Some researchers think that they <u>could have been used</u> to pass on information.

   _____

3.   If you are interested in prehistoric art, Lascaux II can <u>show you what it was like</u>.

   _____

4.   <u>After being discovered</u>, Lascaux became a sensation and was opened to the public in 1948.

   _____


**E**   **Unscramble the words to complete the sentences.**

1.   and found / wall paintings / a cave / they entered / full of

   Together, _____

2.   to enter / scientific experts / the real caves / only a few / are allowed

   _____

3.   leading / there / about a secret tunnel / a legend / to a lost treasure / was

   Long ago, _____

4.   a huge amount / of visitors / of damage / caused / a large number / to the paintings

   _____

MEMO

**MEMO**

Reading for Subject

SECOND
EDITION